HEALTHY RECIPES FOR FAMILIES

To have access to the online French translation and additional content,
scan the QR code below with your smartphone.

*Pour accéder à la traduction française en ligne du livre ainsi qu'à plus de contenu,
scannez le code QR ci-dessous à l'aide de votre smartphone.*

Or enter this URL in your phone or computer's web browser:
consciouscooking.com/healthyrecipesforfamiliesextras

*Ou entrez cet URL dans le navigateur web de votre téléphone
ou ordinateur: consciouscooking.com/healthyrecipesforfamiliesextras*

Printed in the United States of America

First Printing, 2019

ISBN 978-1-7331658-0-8

consciouscooking.com

CONSCIOUS COOKING

HEALTHY RECIPES FOR FAMILIES

MOSTLY GLUTEN- AND DAIRY-FREE • SUPERFOODS • BLW

KRYSTELLE F. GRATZIANI

DEDICATION

To my dear son, Noah; my stepchildren, Mathias, Tristan and Sophia; and all the children in the world, my hope is that you learn to develop the taste and appreciation for real, wholesome foods that nature has provided us everything we need to heal ourselves. Stay open-minded, always keep learning and always listen to your body and heart. I hope that one day you teach your children the same.

To my loving husband, Stephan, thank you for always believing in me and continuously supporting me in achieving my dreams. Nothing would have been possible without you. I love you.

CONTENTS

INTRODUCTION

Do you have memories from when you were a child, coming home from school, and as you open the door and walk into your house, you can smell the aroma of a warm soup cooking on the stove or the sweet smell of cookies baking in the oven? Do you remember being so excited about being given a meal you really enjoyed - or maybe even a special treat – by a loving, caring person in your life? Childhood food memories are soothing to the soul. They feel nostalgic not only because of the food itself and the emotions attached to it, but also because of the whole experience associated to it, like being a family and being nourished.

Cooking is very nurturing, and I believe is so important for families. It creates connections and memories. It's also a practice of mindfulness, an act of altruism and self-care that can be very therapeutic. The person who cooks usually cook with one of the most important, yet invisible ingredients: love. Love is one of the elements that deeply soothes the soul. This is why we sometimes say that food not only nourishes our body but our soul —and mind—as well.

The food we eat has an effect on our entire being. It affects how our body functions, how our mind thinks, and affects our energy and vibration level. Additionally, when we eat with mindfulness and gratitude in a loving and joyful environment, it has a positive effect on our entire well-being. Food interacts with humans on a biological, psychological, spiritual and energetic level. To achieve optimum health, I believe it's important to nourish our

bodies on all levels, rather than just focusing on the food we eat. Food is not only "food".

I created this cookbook because healthy food for children is a subject that is very close to my heart. I believe that every child should predominantly eat nutritious, balanced and homemade meals and be taught healthy eating habits from the beginning. It's one of our responsibilities, as parents, to provide nutritious meals to our children so that they can grow up healthy – physically, mentally and emotionally. This cookbook contains nutritious, nourishing and relatively easy-to-make recipes for your family, including your baby or toddler, to support you in this journey of health and conscious cooking.

This cookbook has been created for you – parents, grandparents and caregivers – who care about your family's health and take pride in nourishing your family with fresh, homemade foods. My hope is that this book helps and inspires you to make nutritious and nurturing meals for your family and that it brings a level of fulfillment into yourself.

With love and good health,

Krystelle

*"Take care of your body.
It's the only place you have to live."*

JIM ROHN

FOOD PHILOSOPHY

Food is one of the greatest joys in life. Unfortunately, in today's world, it can easily become one of the greatest struggles. Food is not only used to satisfy physical hunger but emotional needs as well. Many people turn to food to cope with stress or unpleasant emotions, such as boredom, loneliness, or sadness. Many people also struggle with body image issues or eating disorders. With our busy, fast-paced lifestyle, we eat on the go, we eat out, we eat fast and we eat with distractions, rarely paying attention to what our body needs. Moreover, while we live in a world of abundance, there are still millions of people around the world who are malnourished and struggle with hunger.

I believe education is one of the most powerful tools to empower ourselves and makes a difference in our lives and the world. The education I have acquired through the years has contributed to the food philosophy I have today. Food is nourishment for the body, mind and soul. Therefore, what we consume affects our whole being, so we should choose what we put in our body with care. My food philosophy involves the beliefs of bio-individuality; wholesome foods; local, seasonal, organic and sustainable food; traditional food and preparation techniques; homemade meals; flexibility; and mindful eating.

BIO-INDIVIDUALITY

I believe there is no one perfect way of eating that is suitable for everybody. We are all unique and have different nutritional needs according to our age, gender, size, constitution, lifestyle and ancestry. The goal, in my opinion, is to find what works for us and find the food that makes us feel the most vibrant, energetic and balanced. There is no right or wrong answer – only what's right for us.

With patience, practice and without judgment, we can become more conscious and learn to listen to the messages our body sends us daily in order to reconnect with our body's needs. Doing so can help us find the food we should eat or avoid. It's possible that our diet will change throughout the year or over time. Our bodies are changing constantly – and so are the days, months, seasons and life – so it makes sense that our diet will too.

Although I believe we are all unique and have different dietary needs, I believe we should mostly eat unprocessed, unrefined and wholesome foods.

WHOLESOME FOODS

I believe in natural, wholesome foods. Food that is unrefined, unprocessed and rich in nutrients. These are foods that are as close to their natural state, as nature intended them to be consumed – think of food like fruits, vegetables, root vegetables, leafy greens, herbs, whole grains and pseudo-grains, beans and legumes and nuts and seeds.

If animal proteins are consumed, think of whole eggs, fish, seafood, poultry and meat. If possible, make sure the animals have been humanely raised and have been fed their natural diets.

By eating a balanced diet with a variety of natural whole foods, you eat foods that are nutrient-dense rather than energy-dense. You eat foods that do not contain artificial flavors, added sugar, food coloring or refined vegetable oils. You eat real foods. By doing so, you provide your body the nutrients it needs to thrive.

LOCAL AND SEASONAL

Eating local and seasonal is one of the healthiest ways to eat. When eating locally, you naturally eat what's in season and support your body in its transition throughout the year. You eat foods that are more warming and grounding to the body during winter and foods that are cooler and lighter during summer. By eating locally and seasonally, you not only eat food that is fresh, flavorful and nutritious but also supports local farms and community.

ORGANIC AND SUSTAINABLE

Organic is a labeling term that indicates that the food or product has been produced through approved methods. According to the United States Department of Agriculture, organic producers rely on natural substances and physical, mechanical or biologically based farming methods to the fullest extent possible. Food must be produced without synthetic fertilizers and pesticides, genetic engineering, ionizing radiation or sewage sludge. Animals should not be administered antibiotics or hormones, should be fed 100 percent organic feed and be raised in living conditions accommodating their natural behaviors. Organic processed foods cannot contain artificial preservatives, colors or flavors and must be made with ingredients that are organic.

Sustainable agriculture is the production of food using farming techniques that protect the environment, public health, communities and animal welfare. It's a way of growing food in an ecologically and ethically responsible manner without depleting natural resources. For instance, sustainable agriculture helps to sustain the land by allowing a longer use of the soil for crop rotation. Sustainable farming also uses methods like reclaimed water to ensure that water isn't wasted and incorporates renewable resources like wind, solar or water power. Farmers also care about their animals and provide more space for them to roam as they would naturally have in the wild.

TRADITIONAL FOODS AND PREPARATION TECHNIQUES

Traditional foods are food in their original forms that have been consumed throughout history, such as grass-fed meat, pastured eggs, cod liver oil, ghee, sauerkraut, kefir and bone broth – just to name a few. They are naturally grown or raised, nutrient-dense and thoughtfully prepared. These are the types of food that your grandparents and great-grandparents would have used and recognized today.

Traditional food preparation techniques, such as soaking, sprouting and fermenting, are beneficial for our health – especially with plant foods like grains, legumes and nuts and seeds – as they contain substances like phytic acid and enzyme inhibitors that interfere with the body's ability to absorb nutrients. The process of soaking, sprouting and fermenting reduce those substances, making those foods more digestible and nutritious. Fermentation also improves taste, acts as a natural preservative and provides beneficial bacteria that support digestive and immune health.

Other techniques, such as drying, salt curing and smoking, were traditionally used and meant to improve taste and preserve food.

HOMEMADE MEALS

I truly believe in the importance of homemade meals. Cooking at home is an act of love. It's not only food for the body but also for the mind and soul. When you take the time to cook at home for your family, you make memories, can follow traditions and may even reinforce family bonds. You can take the opportunity to teach your children how to cook or teach them about nutrition, health, gardening or the environment. It's a beautiful way to connect with them while transmitting knowledge and values that will follow them through life. Homemade meals have been proven to make children healthier and happier. Remember, you don't need to be a chef to cook at home. You need a kitchen, food and the desire to cook. Keep it simple when needed. There is a true beauty in simplicity.

Homemade meals are not only nurturing but usually more nutritious, especially when real ingredients are used. When cooking at home, you also have control of the quality and quantity of the ingredients, food preferences, food intolerances and allergies, portion sizes and food safety. It's beneficial in so many ways!

FLEXIBILITY

As much as I'm a big believer in healthy eating, I also believe in the importance of being flexible and enjoying life. Life is not only about food, restraint and control but also about fun, experiences and making memories. Life is too short and beautiful to be too strict with ourselves. It's wonderful to have discipline and eat healthily, but it's also wonderful to enjoy the little things in life. Doing this is healthy too – just in a different way.

I believe it's important to be able to experience certain food in life without the feeling of guilt or shame. Any food can be healthy if eaten occasionally or in moderation. The truth is that there are no good or bad foods – only foods that promote wellness while others don't. The key, in my opinion, is to find balance and balance starts from within. It starts when our thoughts are aligned with our inner being.

MINDFUL EATING

Last but not least, I believe in mindful eating. Mindful eating is being present to the sensations and thoughts that come up as we eat and without judgment or criticism. It helps us to hear what our body is telling us. It also helps us become aware of what our body, mind or soul needs. When we practice mindful eating, we pay attention to what our body is experiencing. We know when we are hungry or thirsty or when we are satisfied. We also pay attention to the smells, flavors, textures and colors of the food that is in front of us.

Mindful eating is also about practicing gratitude – gratitude for the food we have, for the people who prepared the meal for us and even for the farmers who harvested the food for us. When we cultivate healthy thoughts, we affect our whole body positively. We have so much to be grateful for. We can't control everything in life, but we can control how we think. If we can learn to find beauty in any situation of life, I believe it's another beautiful way to remain healthy.

ABOUT THE RECIPES

The recipes you will find in this cookbook do not follow a specific diet or "way of eating" but are, instead, focused on healthy eating. The recipes are made with whole, local, seasonal and mostly organic and unprocessed ingredients. You will find recipes that are entirely free of animal products while you will find some that contain pastured eggs, sustainable fish, organic poultry and grass-fed meat. Herbs and spices, as well as super-foods, are found throughout the book as they increase nutritional value and health benefits of meals. Finally, high-quality, unrefined salt is used in the recipes while sweeteners are natural and unrefined.

The recipes are mostly gluten- and dairy-free. You will find a few recipes that contain sprouted grain bread and pasta, as well as plain, whole-milk yogurt or grass-fed butter, as I believe these foods can be part of a healthy diet. Options are given, however, if you rather avoid them. Many of the recipes are also grain- and soy-free. While some recipes contain them, only the highest quality ingredients are chosen, and alternatives are provided. Many recipes are also nut-free, and these recipes are labeled in the book to make it easier for parents that have children with allergies to identify them.

I have included healthier versions of some of the "classic family meals" and "children's favorites" that are sure to please your family. In addition, there are several international recipes as well, which allow you and your family to add variety and discover new foods and flavor profiles. Most recipes are easy or quick to make, and cooking methods have been chosen to preserve nutrients and support health. In most meals, I have also incorporated some of the food-combining rules to support digestion and overall health.

If you have a baby at home, the recipes follow the baby-led weaning (BLW) approach. However, to make it easier for your baby to eat, you may need to cut the food into smaller pieces or mash the food slightly to aid in the digestion of nutrients. Natural, unrefined salt is used in the recipes. However, if you prefer to omit salt, you may season your dish after serving your baby's portion. There is also a section in the book with more information on this topic and a few recipes that have been created specifically for babies.

New foods or tastes may take time to be enjoyed and appreciated but are worth the effort. Be patient with yourself and your family and just do your best. You will harvest what you plant one day. It's best to start introducing healthy foods as early as possible, but it's never too late to start. Keep in mind that healthy meals don't have to be complicated. In fact, keeping it simple can be just as good, if not better.

Lastly, the best advice I can give you is to focus on using high-quality ingredients and include more fresh, wholesome foods into your diet. I believe that by nourishing your body with fresh, whole-some foods and by using high-quality ingredients, you are taking the very first best steps into achieving a healthier life.

THE IMPORTANCE
OF FATS IN THE DIET

Fats are a very important component of our diet. They are part of every cell membrane and every organ and tissue in the body. They protect our internal organs from trauma and cold, keep our cells strong, and are essential for our nervous system and in the manufacturing of hormones. Fats are also needed for absorption of vitamins A, D, E and K. They also add flavor to foods, provide satiety and are a ready source of energy. Fats are needed for health, but they need to be chosen with care and consumed in moderation.

Infants and growing children benefit from more fat in their diet rather than less. They need fat for proper growth and development, especially for the development of the brain. Some prominent pediatricians have recognized that low-fat diets may develop health and growth problems, and a study has linked low-fat diets with a failure to thrive in children. Human milk provides about 50 percent of its calories as fat, and about half of that comes from saturated fats. It contains antimicrobial fatty acids known as lauric acid and capric acid, which give the infant protection against viruses, bacteria and protozoa. It's also rich in cholesterol.

There are four different types of fats: Monounsaturated, polyunsaturated, saturated and trans fats. While some play several important roles in the body and are needed for health, some should indeed be avoided. Cholesterol, on the other hand, is a different type of fat that is also necessary for optimum health.

Monounsaturated and polyunsaturated fats are classified as the unsaturated fats and are considered the "healthy" fats. Monounsaturated fats have a number of health benefits. They may protect against heart disease, improve cholesterol levels and immune function and lower inflammation. They are found in food like olive oil, macadamia oil, avocados and most nuts. Polyunsaturated fats include the omega-3 and omega-6 fats. These essential fatty acids are needed for proper brain function and cell growth. They are not produced in the body and, therefore, must be obtained through food.

Omega-3 fatty acids are highly beneficial for brain and heart health and reducing inflammation in the body. They are crucial for children, and deficiencies have been associated with both mental and physical health problems as well as learning deficiencies. The best sources of omega-3s are fatty fish like salmon, mackerel and sardines and fish oils like krill and fermented cod liver oil. They can also be found in some plant food like walnuts, flaxseeds, chia seeds, hemp seeds and seaweed, but they are not absorbed in the body as efficiently as the ones found in fish sources.

Omega-6 fatty acids are also beneficial for health and are necessary for normal growth and development but, in excess, they promote inflammation in the body. We only need a small amount of omega-6, and the Western diet is filled with them as they are found in popular food like meat, dairy, eggs, nuts and seeds, vegetable oils and many baked goods and processed foods. Today, most people are eating an excessive amount of omega-6 fatty acids, especially from vegetable oils and processed foods. An excessive amount of omega-6 combined with a very low ratio of omega-3 is suspected to contribute to excess inflammation and the pathogenesis of many diseases involving inflammatory processes. The focus should be on improving omega-3 fat intake and reducing the consumption of vegetable oils and processed foods. A balanced omega-6/omega-3 ratio is vital for health.

Saturated fats, on the other hand, are required for the nervous system to function properly. They are needed for energy, hormone production, cellular membrane, bone health, immune function and much more. While some saturated fats may have a negative effect on our health, it's important to know that not all saturated fats are created equal. They come in different lengths. There are short-, medium- and long-chain fatty acids. Our bodies need all three kinds to remain healthy. For instance, butter is a terrific source of butyric acid, a short-chain fatty acid. Coconut and palm oil, as well as breast milk, contain caprylic, capric and lauric acids, which are medium-chain fatty acids. Both the short- and medium-chain fatty acids have antimicrobial properties and contribute to the health of the immune system. Long-chain fatty acids – myristic, palmitic and stearic acids – can be found in food like palm and coconut oil and cacao butter as well as dairy and animal fats. They are not necessarily unhealthy, but you want to choose high-quality products and consume them in moderation.

Trans fat is the worst type of fat, making it the type that you want to avoid. Trans fat is a byproduct of a process called hydrogenation that is used to turn healthy oils into solids and to prevent them from becoming rancid. It's the type of fat that can increase your risk of heart disease as they increase the levels of "bad" cholesterol and decrease the levels of "good" cholesterol in the body. On food label ingredient lists, trans fat is typically listed as "partially hydrogenated oil." It's the type of fat found in commercially baked and fried foods, such as french fries and donuts. Trans fats are also in margarine, shortening and some snack and convenience foods like cookies, chips, and crackers. To remain healthy, it's important to lower the intake of trans fats.

Cholesterol is a type of fat that is found in food but also in our blood. It plays many vital roles in the body and, without it, the body could not function. It's the basis for the formation of many hormones and vitamins in the body, and it's essential for the brain, and the production of cell membranes and bile. Cholesterol is found in animal foods only. Therefore, plant foods like avocados, potatoes or coconut oil do not contain any cholesterol. Because the body requires a lot of cholesterol, it can make its own. Many people still associate cholesterol with heart diseases. However, it's now known that cholesterol is not the cause of heart disease but rather the damaged or oxidized cholesterol that comes from processed foods or foods that have been heated at high temperature – particularly vegetable oils. Most vegetable oils turn rancid at high temperature or are highly refined to tolerate higher heat.

To conclude, fats are needed for health and are especially important for infants and growing children. We shouldn't fear them but should choose them with care. All foods that are rich in fat contain a combination of fatty acids. Therefore, it's best to consume fats that come from whole foods, such as organic grass-fed meat, wild fish, pastured egg yolks, grass-fed butter, ghee, avocado, raw nuts and seeds, coconut oil, extra-virgin olive oil and cold-pressed flaxseed oil. It's also important to know that pesticides and chemicals are stored in fat cells, so choosing organic, especially for animal products, is very important to avoid chemical exposure. Again, it's best to stay away from refined vegetable oils and processed foods and, of course, balance your fat intake with a variety of fresh fruits and vegetables.

WHAT YOU NEED TO KNOW ABOUT SALT

Salt is a mineral made of sodium and chloride. It has always been an essential part of life on Earth. Not only it's a natural food enhancer and preservative, but it's also essential for human life. Salt is in our tears, our sweat, our blood – it's necessary for the body to function. It supports a host of hormonal, chemical and electrical processes in the body, and its trace minerals are especially important for the health of the heart, brain and adrenal glands. Salt is a major component of the body's fluids. Without salt, our nervous system could not function. In fact, without salt, we could not survive.

Salt is essential to life but needs to be consumed in moderation and preferably come from natural sources like fruits, vegetables and seaweed or unrefined salt. Even though all salts are sodium and chloride, not all salt is created equal. The processing methods alter its taste, color, texture, nutritional value, energy and effects on the body. Therefore, you always want to choose unrefined natural salt and avoid refined commercial table salt.

Commercial table salt is 97.5 percent sodium chloride and 2.5 percent man-made chemicals. It's highly refined. It's chemically produced, bleached and devoid of nutrients. It's heated at very high temperature (1200°F), which alters the natural structure of salt and removes all trace minerals, leaving only sodium and chloride. It contains ingredients like anticaking agents, iodine and other additives. Table salt also contains aluminum, which is known to lead to neurological disorders, particularly when no selenium is provided to help the body to bind it. Table salt can contribute to many health problems such as high blood pressure, heart and kidney disease as well as fluid retention. It should indeed be avoided.

Unrefined salt, on the other hand, is very different. It's 84 percent sodium chloride, and 16 percent naturally occurring trace minerals. Those trace minerals support the brain and nervous system as well as adrenal, immune and thyroid function. Natural salt is the most important component in alkalizing the blood and tissues. It's a natural antihistamine, helps the body eliminate toxins, and remove excess acidity from the brain cells. It supports bone density and circulatory health and balances sodium-potassium ratios. Salt also assists digestion by helping the body to digest and absorb nutrients and balancing blood sugar levels. The best unrefined salts to use are Himalayan, Celtic or Real Salt.

Himalayan salt is harvested from an ancient salt deposit in Khewra, Punjab, in Pakistan. It's believed to be the purest form of salt available. Himalayan salt is hand-mined, hand-washed and minimally processed. It's uncontaminated with toxins or pollutants from the water. Its color, which is the result of its iron content, varies from different shades of pink to deep reds.

Celtic salt is sustainably harvested from the bottom of ponds off the coast of France. Its light gray color comes from the mineral-rich, pure clay lining of the salt beds from which it is harvested. It's unrefined, unwashed and additive-free.

Real Salt is an all-natural salt that comes from an underground salt deposit in Redmond, Utah. It's unrefined, has a complete blend of minerals and a subtle, sweet flavor. It's an environmentally friendly option as it comes from the United States. The company also uses solar panels to power almost all its operations. Real Salt is also the most affordable option.

There are also other varieties of salts to choose from like sea salt, kosher salt, fleur de sel and Hawaiian sea salt. Sea salt is harvested from evaporated seawater, contains some minerals and is less refined than table salt. However, small concentrations of heavy metals and microplastics are found or have been detected in sea salt as it comes from the ocean. Kosher salt is less processed than table salt, has a coarser and larger grain, takes longer to dissolve, does not contain iodine and is suitable for sprinkling on top of meat.

Fleur de sel is hand-harvested from tidal pools off the coast of Brittany, France. It's the most expensive salt and is used as a finishing salt. Hawaiian sea salt can be red or black. The red color comes from mixing native sea salt with an iron oxide-rich volcanic clay, and the black color comes from combining salt with activated charcoal.

Salt is essential for health, but you want to choose wisely and consume in moderation. Invest in a high-quality unrefined salt and, if you are concerned about your salt intake, move toward a healthy diet that contains natural, wholesome foods and limits or avoids processed and refined foods. It's also best to cook at home instead of eating out as you can control the quality and quantity of the ingredients used.

If you have an infant at home and are concerned about salt intake, it's important to know that babies only need tiny amounts of salt (less than 0.4 grams) in their diets and that need is generally met through breast milk or formula. However, a few grains of high-quality, unrefined salt in their food will not do any harm and can indeed be beneficial, especially when no processed foods are eaten. However, because it's a very controversial subject, you may want to stay on the safer side and wait a few more months before adding salt to their food.

"Considered the 5th universal element, pure ocean salt is our physical and spiritual salvation. Containing a wealth of vital minerals, such as magnesium, calcium and iodine, it nurtures our digestion and our thoughts. It draws toxins and stress out of the body while relaxing the mind and is one of the most powerful mineral elements bringing balance to our lives."

SERENA DOUGALL

WHY CHOOSE ORGANIC AND LOCAL FOOD?

First and foremost, let's define what organic foods are. Organic foods are produced without the use of pesticides or chemical fertilizers and are not irradiated or contain genetically modified organisms (GMOs). Organic produce may be more nutritious than conventional produce as the soil in which they grow is richer in nutrients. Organic meat, poultry, eggs and dairy products are produced from healthier animals that have been fed an organic, non-GMO feed; that have not been given any antibiotics or growth hormones; and have much better living conditions. Organic food is also better for the environment as food is produced by farmers who emphasize the use of renewable resources and the conservation of soil and water.

Organic foods are preferable for babies and young children as they are particularly vulnerable to chemical exposure. Their bodies are small and fragile, and their organs are not fully developed yet. Recent research suggests that even low levels of pesticide exposure can affect young children's neurological and behavioral development. Evidence shows a link between pesticides and neonatal reflexes, psychomotor and mental development and attention-deficit hyperactivity disorder. Pesticides have also been shown to affect a variety of body systems, including reproductive, endocrine, immune, and respiratory. Choosing organic food is one of the best ways to reduce chemical exposure. Ideally, education about pesticide exposures should begin prior to pregnancy.

Organic food is costlier than conventional foods. If you are on a budget and wish to buy organic, there are a few things you can do. You can choose to buy mainly fruits and vegetables, which are known to have the highest amounts of pesticides.

You can reduce your consumption of conventional meat and dairy products, cut down on processed foods to buy higher-quality products, buy frozen, buy in bulk or buy organic food only for your children. You can also look for coupons or buy in major grocery store chains, shop at your farmers' market, join a community-supported agriculture program or a food co-op or, even better, have a garden of your own and teach your children how to plant, take care of and harvest plants. Not only it's a terrific way to have high-quality products right at home, but it's also a great opportunity to teach your children, connect with them and build an appreciation for different produce and nature.

Local food, on the other hand, can be just as nutritious – if not better. It depends on the food itself. Eating local food means eating seasonally. Local food is fresher, tastes better and is more nutritious as it gets from the field to your table quickly and, therefore, loses fewer nutrients. Eating local also supports area farms and the local economy, benefits the environment, promotes food safety and helps to build more connected communities. Eating locally and seasonally is also a natural way to stay connected with the cycle of nature and feed our body with what it truly needs.

FRESH, FROZEN AND CANNED FOODS

Fresh fruits and vegetables – especially if coming from a local farm or farmers' market or your garden – will give you the most nutrients and flavors as they are picked at their peak and have not traveled very far. Eating fresh foods usually means eating locally and seasonally, which is a very healthy way of eating as our bodies require different types of foods as the seasons change. Fresh, local foods can even be superior to organic fruits and vegetables.

Frozen fruits and vegetables are also a superb choice as they are frozen right after being harvested, which means that they have kept most of their nutrients and flavors. They are also convenient as the washing and cutting are already done. Keep in mind, however, that there are different factors that influence the nutrients in frozen foods, such as the temperature of the freezing unit, length of storage, cut, thawing method and packaging method. Frozen vegetables don't have to be thawed before cooking.

Most canned foods are processed within hours of harvest so that their nutritional value is preserved. Canned beans and legumes can be particularly convenient as they are cooked prior to packing so that they are ready to eat. Canned fruits and vegetables are still a decent choice. They are better than processed foods or no fruits or vegetables at all. When purchasing canned foods, look for organic products and BPA-free cans and avoid cans with added salt or sugar or fruits that have been packed in syrup.

PESTICIDES ON PRODUCE

Pesticides are used to control pests on produce. Although the definitive effects of the ingestion of pesticides by humans have not been established, there is strong evidence that pesticides harm both those working with and those consuming the produce. Dietary modification is one of the best ways to reduce pesticide exposure. This is particularly important if you are pregnant or breastfeeding, or if you have children. According to the American Academy of Pediatrics, children are especially vulnerable to pesticides due to developmental, dietary, and physiological reasons.

When possible, avoid exposing yourself and your family to pesticides by purchasing the fruits and vegetables listed in the Environmental Working Group's "Dirty Dozen" list from an organic producer.

The following lists are from the EWG's 2019 Shopper's Guide:

DIRTY DOZEN	CLEAN FIFTEEN
(choose organic)	*(conventional is OK)*
Strawberries	Avocados
Spinach	Sweet corn*
Kale	Pineapples
Nectarines	Sweet peas (frozen)
Apples	Onions
Grapes	Papayas*
Peaches	Eggplants
Cherries	Asparagus
Pears	Kiwis
Tomatoes	Cabbages
Celery	Cauliflower
Potatoes	Cantaloupes
	Broccoli
	Mushrooms
	Honeydew Melons

*If you want to avoid genetically modified produce, when buying sweet corn, papaya and summer squash sold in the United States, buy organic. Most Hawaiian papaya and a small percentage of sweet corn, zucchini and yellow squash sold in the United States is genetically modified.

ESTABLISH HEALTHY EATING HABITS FOR YOUR FAMILY

As parents, we should teach our children – as early as possible – to develop healthy eating habits. This way, as they grow, they have a healthy relationship with food, which will impact the rest of their life. It's something that is essential for their physical, mental and emotional health.

Here are 15 ideas on how parents can encourage healthy eating habits for their family:

1. If pregnant, start by eating a healthy, balanced diet. A child's food preference begins in the womb. The tastes and flavors eaten during pregnancy are known to influence the baby's palate.

2. When your children are little, use the opportunity to give them healthy foods. Try not to let them discover processed foods too early. They will find out about them soon enough. Enjoy the early times to try to build the best foundation possible.

3. Explain to your children the importance of eating real foods instead of processed ones. If they are little, you can simply explain how some foods nourish our body and make us feel good and strong and some don't. Make it simple.

4. Try to share at least one meal a day with your family, preferably at the dining table. This helps to bring stability and it's emotionally nourishing. It's also a beautiful way to connect with your family.

5. Avoid any electronics, such as cellphones or TV, at the dining table. Not only it's disrespectful to others, but it can also lead to overeating as you and your family may ignore the food you eat and the feeling of being full.

6. Before a meal, take a deep breath to relax and ground yourself. Pray if you like. Teach the importance of being – and eating – in the present moment.

7. Teach your children to pay attention to the body's signals of hunger, thirst and fullness. It's also important to eat when hungry and emotionally at peace.

8. Explain to your children the reasons why they should be thankful for the food they have and, every so often, take the time to talk about where the food comes from, how and where it grows and how it's harvested and by who.

9. If and when snacks are needed, encourage healthy snacks like fresh fruits, smoothies, homemade granola bars, muffins or crudités with a healthy dip. If they are hungry, they will eat it. Don't encourage snacking when the child is bored.

10. Instead of asking your children what they want to eat, offer them two or three healthy choices. It's fun for the child to be able to choose, and it's a good way to keep control of the food being eaten.

11. Try to avoid giving your child a dessert after every meal. Try to make them available occasionally instead, such as on the weekends, birthday parties or holidays. It's also best if they are homemade – and even better if your kids help you make them.

12. Avoid using food or dessert as a reward, such as when your children finish their plate or for being nice with their sibling. It can create power struggles around eating later on.

13. If your child doesn't like a certain type of food, don't be discouraged. Wait and try again – and again. Be patient. Taste develops over time and children won't develop a taste for healthy food if healthy food is not on their plate. Encourage your child to take at least one bite of the healthy food you make.

14. Acknowledge your children when they eat or choose to eat something healthy. Always try to recognize them for positive behaviors. It will make them want to do it more.

15. Be the parent and be the example. Try to eat healthy as often as possible and encourage your children to do the same. You can even start gardening or involve your children in the kitchen. Kids like to be involved and like to do what grownups do.

BABIES AND TODDLERS

Although all the recipes in the book are meant to be enjoyed by your little ones, this section has been created specifically for them. It contains recipes like banana crepes, prune purée, tropical fruit salad and teething and oatmeal cookies. Those recipes are simpler and contain fewer ingredients.

Whenever possible, use the best quality ingredients possible for your little ones. Although not necessary, a few grains of unrefined salt here or there in your baby's food is acceptable and healthy, especially if no processed foods are eaten. Only use unrefined salt like Himalayan, Celtic or Real Salt – it's very rich in minerals. Never use table salt! Also, remember never to give honey to infants.

INTRODUCTION TO SOLID FOODS

According to the World Health Organization (WHO), infants should be exclusively breastfed for the first 6 months of life to achieve optimal growth, development, and health. The WHO recommends that infants start receiving complementary foods at 6 months of age in addition to breast milk. Food should be nutritionally adequate, prepared properly and given in a safe manner to avoid the risk of contamination.

A newborn who drinks his or her mother's milk receives the perfect food to fulfill his or her needs. Milk is nourishing, soothing to the soul and carries the warmth of life. Breast milk contains all the essential nutrients needed for optimum growth and development and adequate water for hydration. It protects against infection and allergies and contributes to immune maturation, organ development and healthy microbial colonization. Breastfeeding also has a protective effect on infant morbidity. If breastfeeding is not possible, a hypo-allergenic formula is recommended.

Milk, either breast milk or formula, is the main source of nutrition for the entire first year. Cow's milk should not replace breast milk or formula as it does not provide enough nutrition for proper growth. Premature feeding can lead to poor digestion, increased allergy, immune problems, and obesity as well as influence later eating habits. Around 6 months is the typical age when solids should be introduced, although there are a few exceptions.

Infants show signs of readiness when they can hold their necks steady and sit with support, open their mouth in a preparatory way and stop pushing their tongues out when a spoon or food is placed in their mouth. They are also usually ready when they can crawl, have teeth and reach or grab food on plates. Babies show disinterest or fullness by leaning back, turning away, pushing the food out of their mouths, sealing their lips together, playing with food and pushing the bottle or spoon away. Babies should be fed when they are hungry and should never be forced to eat or be on a rigid schedule.

First foods should be simple, natural and preferably organic. It's not necessary to purée food, although puréed food may be easier to digest. Start with what you feel comfortable with. Go slowly and always be observant, especially when introducing common allergens. You may also want to wait a few days after introducing a new food so if there is an allergy or food intolerance, it will be detected more easily. Signs of intolerance include redness around the mouth; gas and stomach pain; irritability, fussiness, and waking throughout the night; constipation and diarrhea; regurgitation of foods; coughing and congestion; skin rashes; or more severe reactions like shock or difficulty breathing.

If your baby does not seem interested in food at first, do not worry. Food before the first year of age is mostly to explore and for fun. Nutritional needs are still met through milk. Simply keep offering foods, varying the flavors and textures until your baby is ready. If you have been feeding your baby purées, you may want to try to offer pieces of food to let your baby be in control. You can start with fruits, vegetables, egg yolks, meat or even home-made bone broth. Cereals do not have to be your baby's first food. In fact, cereals should be one of the last foods to be introduced.

Keep in mind that the nutritional needs of babies are different from those of adults. They need more fat and concentrated sources of calories and nutrients to fuel their rapid growth. Their calories should come from nutritious foods. Offer a variety of food with different colors, tastes and textures. Early introduction of different tastes and textures is a good idea to prevent pickiness later. If your baby does not like a specific food, try that same food again later. It may take many times before your baby likes it, if he or she ever does, so keep trying. Finally, always try to make mealtimes a positive and pleasant experience and, whenever possible, have your meals with your child.

IS YOUR INFANT READY FOR SOLID FOODS?

To respect your child's development, it's very important to wait until your child is ready before introducing solids. Readiness for solid foods is less about age and more about the child's abilities. As a general rule of thumb, your baby is ready for solid foods when he or she displays most of the following behaviors. This typically happens around six months of age but could be a little earlier or later:

- Can sit up well with or without support
- Hold head up unassisted
- Has lost the tongue-thrust reflex that pushes food out of the mouth
- Has a growing appetite
- Showing significant weight gain (birth weight has doubled)
- Interest in food and watching others eating
- Tries to grab food to put in his or her mouth
- Opens mouth when food is coming
- Makes chewing motions
- Can pick up food or small object with thumb and forefinger (pincer grasp)

INFANT CEREAL: SHOULD IT BE YOUR BABY'S FIRST FOOD?

Commercial infant cereal is a processed food invented around the time of the Industrial Revolution as a product of convenience. It was advertised as safe, modern and better than what you could prepare at home. Rice cereals are still recommended by many pediatricians and parents as a first food as it's said to be a low-allergen food, easy to digest and a good source of iron, folic acid and zinc. However, in recent years, rice cereal has become less popular. It's now well known that grains may have somewhat of a detrimental effect and many parents choose to start with whole foods instead.

Most commercial infant cereals are highly processed and made with refined grains. Refined grains are grains that have been milled, a process that removes the bran and germ – the two most nutritious part of the grains – leaving only the endosperm, which is the starchy part of the grain. The endosperm is what baby cereals (and white flour) are made up of. During processing, the whole grain loses most of its vitamins, minerals, fiber, antioxidants and phytochemicals. Furthermore, since the grains are refined, they have a high glycemic index and are digested in the body quickly, which cause a rapid spike in blood sugar. It's been proven that both sugars and refined grains are a cause of inflammation and disease.

Also, since most commercial infant cereals are devoid of nutrients, synthetic vitamins – such as folic acid and iron – are added back into it. Folate, a B vitamin, is beneficial and needed. However, its synthetic form – folic acid – may be harmful when consumed in excess. Consuming folate from natural sources like dark, green, leafy vegetables and other plant foods is best. Iron, on the other hand, is a difficult mineral to add to food and is less absorbable, so it's best to consume iron through natural foods like meat, poultry, liver, fish and egg yolks or plant foods like beans, lentils and spinach. However, when consuming iron through plant foods, it's best to consume vitamin C rich foods like fruits and vegetables at the same time to increase its absorption. There has been a long-standing debate on whether synthetic vitamins are as good as natural vitamins. However, most people would agree that the best way to get your nutrients comes from consuming whole foods.

Another area of potential concern is the presence of arsenic in rice. Rice is a leading dietary source of inorganic arsenic, which is a potent carcinogen. It has higher levels than other foods mostly because rice grows in water and tend to absorb arsenic more readily than other food crops. According to the United States Food and Drug Administration (FDA), long-term arsenic exposure is associated with higher rates of skin, bladder and lung cancers as well as heart disease. Choosing brown rice doesn't resolve the issue as it contains more arsenic and whether rice is grown using conventional or organic methods does not affect its arsenic content. Arsenic is also found in other rice products like rice pasta, rice cakes, cereals, and energy bars. However, rice doesn't have to be eliminated completely from the diet but should be consumed in moderation and balanced with other whole foods. The FDA even recommends that rice cereals shouldn't be the only source of fortified cereal and doesn't have to be the first one.

Additionally, other concerns about infant cereals include the lack of amylase in infants and the presence of phytic acid in grains. Amylase is the enzyme needed to digest grains. Infants do produce small amounts of amylase but not in quantities large enough to digest grains properly until they are at least one year old, and it can take up to two years. Improperly digested grains may affect the intestinal lining, disrupt the balance of good bacteria in the gut and create inflammation, which can affect the immune system and lead to food intolerances and allergies. This is one of the reasons why many health experts now recommend waiting at least one year before introducing grains. Phytic acid, on the other hand, is an antinutrient found in grains that blocks the absorption of certain minerals in the body and interferes with digestion. Phytic acid can, however, be reduced significantly by soaking, sprouting or mildly fermenting the grains, which are the traditional ways to prepare whole grains.

Processed baby cereal is also a bland, tasteless food, which can influence later food choices negatively. It's very well-known now that there is absolutely no need to provide bland, tasteless food to babies, and especially to breastfed babies, as they are used to the many different flavors from their mother's milk. It's best to introduce different flavors to your baby so that they are more likely to grow up enjoying different kind of healthy food. In fact, studies show babies' food preferences actually start in utero.

If you want to give cereals to your infant, consider buying organic, alternating grains and making your own cereals at home using high-quality ingredients and cooking methods. By doing so, you will provide a variety of nutrients, textures and flavors. Also, if you make your own cereals, make sure to provide your baby with good sources of iron as the cereals you will be making won't be fortified. But, again, a baby's first food doesn't have to be cereal. A better option would be to start with whole foods, such as avocado, sweet potato, egg yolks or homemade bone broth, or to introduce the healthy food that the parents are eating. Moreover, the most important thing you can do is provide your baby a wide variety of wholesome foods.

WHAT IS BABY-LED WEANING?

Although infants are traditionally introduced to solid foods using spoon-feeding, baby-led weaning, an alternative approach to spoon-feeding, has grown in popularity in recent years. If you are not familiar with this approach, baby-led weaning is about letting your infant be in charge. It means no purées or spoon-feeding. The baby learns to feed himself or herself right from the start of weaning – at about 6 months of age. The baby chooses what, how much and how quickly to eat. He or she is given the freedom to explore new tastes and textures, touch and "play" with food, eats at his or her own pace and stops when he or she has had enough. There is no pressure to eat. The baby leads the whole process, using his or her instincts and abilities, which encourage both confidence and independence.

Babies who are allowed to feed themselves learn about the look, smell, taste and texture of different foods and how distinct flavors work together, rather than having everything puréed together. They also learn how to handle food and manage different textures, sizes and shapes, which supports the child's motor development, such as hand-eye coordination and chewing. Infants who feed themselves also form a natural enjoyment of food, which may reduce the risk of pickiness later on in life.

Letting your baby be in charge is favorable for both the baby and the family. Families feel encouraged together, and one of the reasons behind this is that babies learn by observation and imitation. It also makes mealtime a fun and positive experience, which is likely to give the child a healthy attitude toward food later in life. Parents can also enjoy their own food too as the baby eats right along with them. Baby-led weaning can be very messy, but this stage is quite short and the baby has the chance to practice with food.

Start with foods that are easy to pick up and hold, and cut the food into manageable, bite-sized pieces, strips or sticks. Consider giving large, whole pieces of food if there are no risks of choking. Nonfinger foods, such as oatmeal and yogurt, can be offered with a spoon so your baby can learn to self-feed with a spoon. Depending on the meal served, sugar and salt content should be taken into consideration. You may want to avoid or reduce the amount in a recipe, choose high-quality ingredients or add seasonings after serving your baby's portion. When eating, make sure your infant is always seated upright in a supportive high chair.

Lastly, it's important never to force a baby to eat or take a "last bite." Food offered before the age of 1 is to introduce the baby to new textures and flavors and provide opportunities to learn how to chew and swallow food. Milk, whether its breast milk or formula, remains your baby's primary nutrition source for the entire first year. If your child doesn't seem ready, enjoy the process or eat enough, you can always try later. In the meantime, try to include some puréed foods periodically.

BABY FOOD: COOKING, STORING, REHEATING AND FOOD SAFETY

COOKING

The best cooking method to preserve nutrients is steaming. There are many different steamer baskets on the market. If you don't have one, you can simply place a metal colander over a pot of boiling water. Cook until tender and avoid overcooking to preserve nutrients. Baking and stewing are also excellent methods to preserve flavors and nutrients. Boiling is the least favorable. If you use the boiling cooking method, use the smallest amount of water possible – just enough to cover the food. Avoid overcooking and, if making a purée, thin the food by using the cooking water.

PURÉEING

If you are making purées, avoid overcooking the food and wait until it has cooled down before adding it to your blender or food processor. A food mill can also be used. Nowadays, you can even find devices that allow you to bake and purée your baby's food in the same machine. They can be convenient if you are planning to make many purées but unnecessary if you are planning to do baby-led weaning. If you want texture in your purée, simply use a fork or a food masher.

REFRIGERATING

Immediately after cooking, allow the food to cool down and store it in the refrigerator in a clean, secure safe container with a tightly fitting lid, preferably made from stainless steel or glass. If creating many portions, make individual servings. Do not let food sit at room temperature for more than two hours. To keep food safe, make sure the temperature of your refrigerator is at 40°F or below.

To keep freshness and reduce risks of contamination, use fruit and vegetable meals within 48 hours, and meat, poultry, fish and egg yolk-based meals within 24 hours. Never refrigerate food that has been reheated or if your baby has not finished it. Discard all uneaten baby food.

FREEZING

Before freezing a meal or puréed food, make sure everything has cooled down completely. For small portions, you can use BPA-free ice cube trays to freeze food or multiportion containers that vary in size. Never use glass containers unless labeled for freezing. Make sure the temperature of your freezer is at 0°F or below. Once the food is frozen, take the food out of its container and store it in a well-sealed freezer bag. Don't forget to label the content and add an expiration date. For optimal quality and nutrient retention, use your baby food within one month. Always freeze fresh foods. Do not freeze food from the refrigerator or leftovers. Do not refreeze food that has been previously frozen.

REHEATING

If your food is frozen, you need to defrost it before reheating it. Defrost food in the refrigerator, under cold running water or in the microwave using the defrost setting. Do not defrost by leaving food at room temperature or in standing water. Use thawed food within 48 hours from the time it was removed from the freezer.

To reheat food, you can use the stove top or microwave. I personally favor the stove top as I find it to be the healthiest, tastiest and most effective.

When reheating food, reheat to an internal temperature of 165°F to destroy any bacteria that may be present. Stir food to avoid hot spots and allow to cool before serving to your baby. You want the food to be warm but not hot. Never reheat food more than once. If your baby does not finish the meal, discard any leftovers.

FOOD SAFETY

Infants are at a higher risk of getting a foodborne illness than older children, so it's important to follow some food safety guidelines:

- Always wash your hands thoroughly before preparing baby food and make sure that any equipment used to prepare the food is clean.
- Wash fresh fruits and vegetables thoroughly under clean, running water.
- Use separate cutting boards for meat, poultry and fish and nonmeat foods to avoid cross-contamination.

- Do not use cutting boards with crevices and cuts. Wash and sanitize boards after each use. Plastic cutting boards are especially ideal for animal proteins.
- Use a meat thermometer to cook meat. Red meats should have an internal temperature of at least 160°F, white meat an internal temperature of at least 170°F and dark meat and poultry an internal temperature of at least 180°F for doneness. Cook fish to an internal temperature of 160°F.
- Store meat, poultry and fish in the coldest part of the refrigerator and on the bottom shelf to avoid cross-contamination. Do not allow them to sit out at room temperature.
- Do not leave food (uncooked or cooked) out on the counter at room temperature or between 40° and 140°F for more than two hours.
- Your refrigerator should be set at a temperature of 40°F or below, and your freezer should be 0°F or below.

INFANT'S FIRST FOOD IDEAS

The very first foods eaten by your infant should be easy to digest and unlikely to provoke an allergic reaction. You may want to start with fruits or vegetables, animal proteins like pastured egg yolks or grass-fed meat. Homemade bone broth is also an excellent first "food" as it's extremely nourishing and helps seal the gut lining, thereby strengthening the digestive and immune system. Bone broth can be given with a syringe or put into a cup. When using animal proteins, it's always best to use organic, grass-fed or pasture-raised products. It's very important to feed your growing baby with the best quality food possible. Keep in mind that baby cereals don't have to be your child's first food; there are definitely more nutritious options out there. They key, however, is to provide your child a variety of healthy foods. Also, you can choose whether or not to purée the food but it's not necessary after the baby is six months old.

HERE ARE SOME GREAT FIRST FOOD IDEAS:

- Homemade chicken bone broth
- Egg yolk, preferably from pastured chickens, lightly boiled
- Organic liver, steamed or boiled or frozen for 14 days, and then grated onto foods
- Puréed meats – chicken, beef, lamb, liver, and fish
- Fermented foods – organic grass-fed kefir or yogurt, taro, and cultured vegetable juice
- Cooked vegetables – beets, broccoli, carrots, parsnip, peas, rutabaga, squash, sweet potato, and zucchini
- Raw fruits – avocado, ripe banana (with brown spots on it), papaya, and mango
- Cooked fruits – apples, apricots, peaches, and pears

FOODS TO AVOID

Avoid feeding your infant:

- Processed and refined foods
- Fried foods
- Margarine and shortening
- Sugar
- Table salt
- High-fructose corn syrup
- White flour
- Fish high in mercury, such as swordfish, shark, king mackerel and tilefish
- Commercial, sweetened and/or low-fat dairy products
- Refined soy foods
- Soft drinks
- Fruit juice

Never feed your infant:

- Honey
- Outdated canned foods
- Food from dented, rusted, bulging, leaking or unlabeled cans or jars

Be careful with food that may cause choking like:

- Raw, hard vegetables
- Corn kernels
- Popcorn
- Whole grapes, berries, cherries, melon balls or cherry tomatoes (cut them into quarters)
- Uncooked dried fruits, such as raisins (they are usually fine in porridge as they get softer)
- Nuts

COMMON ALLERGENS

Always use caution when introducing common allergens. When and if you include them, add them one at a time, and wait a few days before introducing another one. Do not mix these foods with new foods. This way, if there is an allergic reaction, the allergen can be identified easily. Some common allergens to watch out for include:

- Gluten
- Dairy products
- Soy
- Citrus
- Tomatoes
- Strawberries
- Egg whites
- Peanuts
- Nuts, including nut butters

BANANA CREPES

SERVES 1-2

PREP 2 minutes   COOK 6 minutes   TOTAL 8 minutes

(💧) NUT-FREE

Your little one will devour these banana crepes. They are such a tasty treat! You can either blend or mash the ingredients together, depending if you want the crepes smooth or slightly chunky, before cooking them in a nonstick skillet over low heat. They are very tasty on their own, but can be served with fresh fruit as well.

INGREDIENTS

½ medium ripe banana, peeled and chopped
1 pastured egg (or 2 egg yolks)
Pinch ground cinnamon
Coconut oil or grass-fed butter, for cooking
1 tablespoon creamy almond butter (optional)

Pure maple syrup, honey, fresh fruits, yogurt
   or chia jam, to serve (optional)

NOTES

If you are concerned about egg allergies for your baby, start by using egg yolks only as they are less likely to provoke an allergic reaction.

INSTRUCTIONS

1. Put banana, egg and cinnamon, and almond butter if using, in a small blender and blend until smooth. Alternatively, for chunkier crepes, mash banana with a fork in a small bowl, add egg, cinnamon, and almond butter if using, and mix to combine.

2. Melt coconut oil or butter in a large nonstick skillet over low heat.

3. Pour small amounts of the batter into the skillet, about 1 tablespoon, trying not to have your crepes touching each other.

4. Cook until the crepes are set and the edges start to change color, about 3 minutes. Then, flip the crepes over and heat until cooked through, about 1 minute more.

5. Serve the crepes by themselves or with a little pure maple syrup, berries, plain yogurt or chia jam.

CARROT PARSNIP FRITTERS

SERVES 4

PREP 15 minutes   COOK 15 minutes   TOTAL 30 minutes

🥜 NUT-FREE

These vegetable fritters are made with carrots, parsnips, red onion and chickpea flour and pan-fried until slightly crisp. They are lovely paired with a dip like hummus or baba ghanoush.

INGREDIENTS

1 cup grated carrots (about 2 medium)
1 cup grated parsnip (about 2 large)
¼ cup grated red onion (about ½ medium)
1 pastured egg
¼ cup chickpea flour
2 tablespoons minced parsley or cilantro
½ teaspoon ground cumin
¼ teaspoon paprika
½ teaspoon unrefined salt
Freshly ground black pepper
Coconut, avocado or olive oil, for frying

INSTRUCTIONS

1. Put carrots, parsnips and red onion in a colander and squeeze out excess water with your hands. Transfer to a large mixing bowl.
2. Stir in egg, chickpea flour, parsley, cumin, paprika, salt, and black pepper. Mix to combine.
3. In a large skillet, heat oil over medium-low heat.
4. Form small patties with a spoon and add them to the skillet, leaving a little bit of space between patties. Cook patties on both sides until warm and crisp, about 3 to 4 minutes on each side. Transfer patties onto a plate lined with paper towel to drain excess oil. Repeat with remaining batter.
5. Serve patties with a dip and a side dish.

BANANA AVOCADO PUDDING

SERVES 1-2

PREP 5 minutes   TOTAL 5 minutes

(Ⓝ) NUT-FREE

This creamy, raw banana avocado pudding is packed with potassium, magnesium and healthy fats. Add raw almond butter or hemp seeds for extra nutrients. For older babies or toddlers, you can even make a smoothie out of it by doubling the recipe and adding a little more water.

INGREDIENTS

½ small ripe banana
¼ avocado
Pinch ground cinnamon
2-3 tablespoons filtered water, to achieve desired consistency
1 teaspoon raw almond butter (optional)
Raw shelled hemp seeds, to garnish (optional)

INSTRUCTIONS

1. Add banana, avocado, cinnamon, almond butter (if using), and water to a blender and blend until smooth.
2. Transfer to a small bowl, garnish with hemp seeds, if desired, or fill a reusable pouch.

NOTE

Almond butter may cause an allergic reaction so when trying for the first time, so only add a very small amount. If tree nut allergies run in your family, you may want to introduce nut butters when your baby is a little older.

DRIED PRUNE PURÉE

SERVES 2-4

PREP 5 minutes   TOTAL 5 minutes

🥜 NUT-FREE

Dried prunes are an excellent source of fiber and various minerals that ensure healthy bowel movement. When blended with banana, this nutritious velvety purée is created and should be enjoyed by your little one. Make sure your banana is ripe.

INGREDIENTS

4 dried prunes, pitted
¼ cup filtered water
½ ripe banana

INSTRUCTIONS

1. Soak prunes overnight in filtered water.
2. In the morning, put prunes, soaking water and banana in a small blender and blend until smooth. If needed, add a little more water to achieve the consistency your baby can handle.
3. Serve a small portion immediately and refrigerate leftovers for later use.

NOTE

A banana is only ripe when there are dark spots on the skin. When ripe, it's easy to digest and is not constipating. Bananas are a good source of dietary fiber as well as vitamin C and potassium.

GARDEN SCRAMBLED EGG

SERVES 1

PREP 2 minutes   COOK 4 minutes   TOTAL 6 minutes

🥜 NUT-FREE

Pastured eggs are a perfect food for your growing baby. While the white is rich in protein, the yolk is the most nutritious part, containing vitamins A, D and E as well as iron, selenium and choline. Choline plays a strong role in human brain development. If you are concerned about an egg allergy, start with the yolk only.

INGREDIENTS

¼ teaspoon extra-virgin olive oil or grass-fed butter
1 pastured egg or 2 egg yolks
1½ tablespoons finely diced mixed vegetables (like onions, bell pepper and zucchini)
A few grains of unrefined salt (optional)

INSTRUCTIONS

1. Warm butter or oil in a medium skillet over medium-low heat.
2. Add diced vegetables, sprinkle with a few grains of salt, if desired, and cook until vegetables are softened, about 2 to 3 minutes.
3. Add the egg and scramble constantly with a spatula until almost cooked through.
4. Transfer scrambled egg to baby's tray or plate. Serve warm but not hot.

SALMON BITES

YIELDS 10 bites

PREP 10 minutes   COOK 20 minutes   TOTAL 30 minutes

Ⓝ NUT-FREE

Made from canned wild Alaskan salmon, these healthy salmon bites are budget-friendly, nutritious, and easy to make. They are delicious served with baked sweet potato fries and steamed broccoli or sliced avocado and sauerkraut for a more complete meal.

INGREDIENTS

1 can (7.5 ounces/213 grams) wild Alaskan salmon, drained and flaked

1 pastured egg, lightly beaten

2 scallions, thinly sliced

1 tablespoon extra-virgin olive oil

1 tablespoon minced fresh dill or cilantro

1 teaspoon lemon zest

1 teaspoon Dijon mustard

¼ teaspoon unrefined salt

⅛ teaspoon ground black pepper

INSTRUCTIONS

1. Preheat oven to 350F.
2. Line a large baking sheet with parchment paper. Set aside.
3. In a large bowl, add salmon, egg, scallions, olive oil, dill, lemon zest, mustard, salt and black pepper. Mix until well combined.
4. Form small bites from the salmon mixture and place them on the baking sheet.
5. Bake for 20 minutes. Serve warm or at room temperature.

TROPICAL FRUIT SALAD

SERVES 2-4

PREP 10 minutes   TOTAL 10 minutes

Ⓝ NUT-FREE

The key to making a naturally sweet fruit salad without adding extra juice or sugar is to use ripe ingredients. The fruits should be soft to the touch, and the banana should have brown spots on it. Cut fruits in very small pieces and mix well before serving. Serve it for breakfast or as a snack and, if you like, mix it with organic plain yogurt or cottage cheese.

INGREDIENTS

1 navel orange, sectioned and chopped
1 ripe mango, pitted and finely chopped
2 ripe kiwis, peeled and finely chopped
1 small ripe banana, finely chopped

INSTRUCTIONS

1. Place all fruits in a bowl, stir well and serve immediately or refrigerate for later use. Serve at room temperature.

NOTE

Feel free to add small chunks of papaya if in season.

NATURAL TEETHING COOKIES

YIELDS 16 cookies

PREP 10 minutes   COOK 20 minutes   TOTAL 30 minutes

🍽 NUT-FREE

Made with all-natural ingredients, these teething cookies are nutritious and great for babies. There's no need to buy packaged cookies any-more. You can now make yours in less than 30 minutes!

INGREDIENTS

2 cups organic, gluten-free rolled oats or 1½ cup oat flour
1 tablespoon ground flaxseeds
1 medium ripe banana
2 tablespoons melted coconut oil
2 tablespoons pure maple syrup
¼ teaspoon ground cinnamon
Pinch unrefined salt

INSTRUCTIONS

1. Preheat oven to 350F and line a baking sheet with parchment paper. Set aside.
2. Turn oats into flour using a food processor or high-speed blender.
3. Add flaxseeds, banana, coconut oil, maple syrup, cinnamon and salt to food processor or blender and pulse a few times to form the dough. Use a rubber spatula to scrape down the sides of the bowl as needed. You can also mix everything in a bowl by mashing the banana with a fork and adding in the rest of the ingredients to form the dough.
4. Remove dough from food processor or blender and place on cookie sheet. Press down gently with your hands and form a square, about ½-inch thick and cut smaller squares out of the dough using a butter knife or bench knife.
5. Bake for 20 minutes or until edges are slightly golden. The cookies will be tender at first but will harden when cooled down. Store in an airtight container.

NOTE

If you rather not use maple syrup, replace by using coconut oil instead.

4-INGREDIENT OATMEAL COOKIES

YIELDS 9 cookies

PREP 5 minutes   COOK 15 minutes   TOTAL 20 minutes

Ⓝ NUT-FREE

Naturally sweetened with banana and cinnamon, these sugar-free cookies are sure to please your little one. Add ground flaxseeds for some extra nutrition.

INGREDIENTS

½ cup gluten-free rolled oats
1 medium ripe banana, mashed
1 tablespoon softened coconut oil
⅛ teaspoon ground cinnamon
1 teaspoon ground flaxseeds (optional)

INSTRUCTIONS

1. Preheat oven to 350F and line a small cookie sheet with parchment paper. Set aside.
2. Add oats to a small blender or food processor and pulse a few times to break them down in smaller pieces. Be careful not to turn them into flour.
3. Mash banana with a fork in a small mixing bowl.
4. Add oats, coconut oil, cinnamon, and flaxseeds, if using, to the bowl with the mashed banana and mix to combine.
5. Spoon out 1 tablespoon of the mixture and place on the cookie sheet. Use a fork and press down on each cookie gently – cookies won't spread when baked.
6. Bake until edges are slightly golden, about 12 to 15 minutes.

NOTE

A similar but more complete cookie recipe can be found on page 283.

STRAWBERRY BANANA YOGURT DROPS

YIELDS 1½ cups

PREP 10 minutes   TOTAL 10 minutes

Ⓝ NUT-FREE

Your little one will enjoy these natural yogurt drops made with Greek yogurt, strawberries and banana. Not only they taste good, but they are also refreshing and wonderful to soothe painful gums caused by teething. For toddlers, feel free to add a little natural sweetener for a slightly sweeter treat.

INGREDIENTS

¼ cup finely chopped strawberries, preferably fresh, or frozen and thawed
½ ripe banana
½ cup organic plain Greek yogurt
1 teaspoon organic honey, maple syrup or coconut nectar (optional)

INSTRUCTIONS

1. Line a baking sheet with parchment paper. Set aside.
2. Put strawberries and banana in a small blender with sweetener, if using, and blend until smooth.
3. Add yogurt to blender and stir gently with a spoon. Do not blend everything together; otherwise, it will be too runny.
4. Transfer mixture to a dispenser bottle, plastic pastry bag or resealable plastic bag with a small corner cut open.
5. Make small drops on the baking sheet, using all the yogurt mixture.
6. Transfer baking sheet to freezer and freeze until set.
7. Transfer drops into a labeled bag or container. Keep in the freezer.

NOTE

For a dairy-free option,
use coconut or almond yogurt.

FROZEN PURÉED CUBES

Frozen puréed cubes are usually enjoyed by babies as they are refreshing, naturally sweet and good for teething. All you need is a BPA-free ice cube tray and a mesh feeder. Simply make the cubes and store them in the freezer into labeled bags or containers. When ready to use, take a cube out, break it if needed, put it into the mesh feeder and give it to your baby to enjoy. You can get creative but here are a few ideas to get you started.

MANGOES

Mangoes are packed with vitamins A and C and make a naturally sweet treat for your little one. Take a fresh mango, peel it and remove the flesh. Put into a small blender and blend until smooth. Pour into an ice cube tray and freeze until set.

WATERMELON

Watermelon is very hydrating and makes a perfect summer treat. Blend the flesh of a piece of watermelon in your blender and pour the juice into an ice cube tray. Freeze until set. You can also try with cantaloupe or honeydew.

STRAWBERRIES

Get organic or local strawberries, wash them and remove the stems. Add them to a blender, blend until smooth and put into an ice cube tray. Freeze until set.

COCONUT MILK

Open a young Thai coconut. Put the coconut water in a blender, then scoop out the flesh and add to the blender as well, making sure there are no hard coconut pieces in the blender. Blend until smooth and pour coconut purée into an ice cube tray. Freeze until set.

BREAST MILK

Put pumped breast milk into an ice cube tray and freeze until set.

BREAKFAST

Breakfast is said to be the most important meal of the day – I believe so too. In the next few pages, you will find a variety of breakfast recipes that will give you a great start to your day. Smoothies and egg recipes will be found in another chapter of the book.

Some recipes suggest to use soaked nuts. To do so, add them to a jar and cover with water. Let sit for a few hours or overnight. In the morning, drain and rinse them, and add them to your breakfast. This process makes them more nutritious and easier to digest.

It's also always best to use homemade milk for the recipes. Otherwise, get the unsweetened versions from the grocery store.

ACAI BOWL WITH MANGOES AND BLUEBERRIES

SERVES 1

PREP 5 minutes   TOTAL 5 minutes

NUT-FREE

Acai is a dark purple berry harvested from acai palm trees which are native to the rainforests of South America. Acai bowls are very popular nowadays. They are refreshing, nutritious, versatile and very pleasant to eat. Plus, they are full of antioxidants and fiber. Enjoy this creamy smoothie bowl with any toppings you like.

INGREDIENTS

½ cup coconut or almond milk
½ medium banana
½ cup frozen mangoes
½ cup frozen blueberries
1 pack (100 grams/3.5 ounces) frozen
    unsweetened acai berry pulp

OPTIONAL TOPPINGS

½ banana, sliced
Fresh fruits like mangoes and kiwis
Nut and seeds like walnuts and chia seeds
Spoonful almond butter
Coconut flakes
Granola
Drizzle of honey or coconut nectar

INSTRUCTIONS

1. Add the coconut milk, banana, frozen mangoes and blueberries to a high-speed blender.
2. Before opening the acai pack, run it under water for a few seconds to thaw it slightly and break it down into smaller pieces. It will make blending easier.
3. Open the pack and add acai pulp into the blender. Start at slow speed and increase the speed slowly until on high, then blend until smooth.
4. Pour into a bowl with a spatula and top with your favorite toppings.

NOTE

If you can't find frozen acai berry, acai berry powder will work just fine. Use about 1 tablespoon per bowl. You may also need to increase the amount of frozen fruits slightly.

AMARANTH PORRIDGE

SERVES 2-4

PREP 5 minutes   COOK 20 minutes   TOTAL 25 minutes

Ⓝ NUT-FREE

Although eaten like a grain, amaranth is not actually a grain. Rather, it is the seed of the amaranth plant. It's a complete source of protein and a rich source of fiber and minerals. Amaranth makes wonderful porridges and is a terrific food to eat during fall and winter. It's a warming, hearty and very nourishing seed. Finish the porridge with your favorite toppings.

INGREDIENTS

¼ cup amaranth
¾ cup water
¼ cup unsweetened almond or coconut milk
½ tablespoon pure maple syrup
¼ teaspoon vanilla extract
⅛ teaspoon ground cinnamon

OPTIONAL TOPPINGS
Fresh fruits, diced or shredded
Dried fruits
Nuts and seeds
Nut butter

INSTRUCTIONS

1. Combine water and amaranth in a small saucepan. Stir, bring to a boil, reduce heat to low, cover, and simmer until water is all absorbed, about 15 minutes.
2. Stir in almond milk, maple syrup, vanilla and cinnamon. Cover again and let simmer until thick and creamy, about 5 minutes.
3. Turn off heat, stir, and pour porridge into bowls. Top with your favorite toppings. Serve warm.

AVOCADO TOAST

SERVES 1-2

PREP 5 minutes TOTAL 5 minutes

Ⓘ NUT-FREE

If you like avocados, you will enjoy this recipe. Your favorite healthy bread is toasted and topped with mashed avocado, a drizzle of extra-virgin olive oil, a splash of fresh lemon juice, a sprinkle of coarse salt and freshly ground black pepper. To make this dish stand out, use a high-quality olive oil and unrefined salt. It makes an excellent breakfast or lunch.

INGREDIENTS

2 slices sprouted, sourdough, or gluten-free bread, toasted
1 small ripe avocado
1 teaspoon extra-virgin olive oil
½ lemon
Celtic, fleur de sel, kosher or Himalayan salt, to taste
Freshly ground black pepper, to taste

INSTRUCTIONS

1. Spread avocado on your favorite healthy toasted bread.
2. Drizzle with olive oil, add a splash of fresh lemon juice, and top with a sprinkle of salt and black pepper.

NOTE

For variation, you can try adding red pepper flakes, fresh herbs, chopped cherry tomatoes or even a fried egg on top for extra protein.

BLUEBERRY BANANA BAKED OATMEAL

SERVES 6

PREP 5 minutes   COOK 45 minutes   TOTAL 50 minutes

Perfect to make for brunch or to feed a large family or crowd, this baked oatmeal made with fruits, nuts and coconut sugar should please everyone. It's warm, comforting and truly delicious.

INGREDIENTS

2 cups gluten-free rolled oats

½ cup coconut flakes, unsweetened

½ cup coconut sugar, sucanat or organic brown sugar

½ cup chopped walnuts

2 tablespoons flaxseeds

1 teaspoon ground cinnamon

¼ teaspoon unrefined salt

2½ cups almond milk, unsweetened

1 teaspoon vanilla extract

1 cup wild blueberries, fresh or frozen

1 ripe banana, sliced

Pure maple syrup, to serve (optional)

INSTRUCTIONS

1. Preheat your oven to 350F.
2. Combine oats, coconut flakes, coconut sugar, walnuts, flaxseeds, cinnamon and salt in a large mixing bowl, and give it a stir.
3. Stir in almond milk and vanilla, then add in blueberries and banana. Stir gently to combine.
4. Pour mixture into a large baking dish.
5. Bake for 45 minutes or until the edges look slightly golden.
6. Serve warm with a drizzle of maple syrup if you like.

BIRCHER MUESLI

SERVES 2

PREP 5 minutes   TOTAL 5 minutes plus chill time

(🥜) NUT-FREE

Muesli is a meal that reminds me of my trips to Europe, as it is served in many European hotels. Muesli is usually made with milk, but I have substituted organic, plain yogurt as it is fermented and therefore healthier. For a dairy-free option, use a plain, nondairy yogurt, such as coconut or almond.

INGREDIENTS

1 small apple
1 cup organic plain yogurt or nondairy yogurt
¼ cup gluten-free rolled oats
2 tablespoons sultana raisins
1 tablespoon sunflower or hemp seeds
1 tablespoon raw, organic or local honey
1 teaspoon flax seeds
¼ teaspoon ground cinnamon
⅛ teaspoon ground nutmeg
Fresh fruit, to serve

INSTRUCTIONS

1. Peel and shred the apple. Squeeze water out with your hands and put apple in a small glass container or bowl.
2. Add yogurt, oats, apple, raisins, sunflower seeds, honey, flaxseeds, cinnamon and nutmeg. Stir well. Cover and refrigerate overnight.
3. In the morning, pour into a bowl, top with fresh fruit and enjoy.

CHIA PUDDING

SERVES 1

PREP 5 minutes   TOTAL 5 minutes plus chill time

🥜 NUT-FREE

Chia puddings make for an excellent breakfast or snack. They are nutritious and easy to make as they don't require any cooking. They can be made in the morning or the night before. It's also an excellent food for babies as it's easy to swallow and digest. Serve the chia pudding on its own or with your favorite add-ins.

INGREDIENTS

2 tablespoons chia seeds
¾ cup nondairy milk (preferably homemade or unsweetened)

OPTIONAL ADD-INS

Fresh berries or seasonal fruits
Dried berries, such as goji berries, golden berries or mulberries
Sliced almonds, pumpkin seeds or hemp seeds
Coconut flakes
Ground cinnamon

INSTRUCTIONS

1. Put chia seeds in a small bowl and add milk. Stir with a spoon to combine, trying to have all the seeds soaked in the milk.
2. Wait about 5 minutes or until the seeds have absorbed all the milk, stir again, add your favorite add-ins if desired, and enjoy.

NOTE

If making the night before, combine chia seeds and milk in a container or jar. Stir, cover and refrigerate overnight. In the morning, add any add-ins that you want and serve. You may also need to add a little more milk to achieve your desired consistency.

FRENCH TOAST

SERVES 2-4

PREP 10 minutes   COOK 5 minutes   TOTAL 15 minutes

Ⓝ NUT-FREE

Most people grew up eating French toast, at least in North America. This pleasurable breakfast item is lovely on a Sunday morning or when having friends over. This recipe will give you the almost same result but in a much healthier version as it uses higher-quality ingredients.

INGREDIENTS

2 pastured eggs, beaten
2 tablespoons coconut sugar
½ teaspoon vanilla extract
¼ teaspoon ground cinnamon
⅛ teaspoon ground nutmeg
Pinch unrefined salt
½ cup nondairy milk, unsweetened
4 slices sprouted, whole-grain or gluten-free bread
Coconut oil or grass-fed butter, for cooking

OPTIONAL TOPPINGS
Pure maple syrup
Sliced banana
Fresh berries

INSTRUCTIONS

1. Whisk together the eggs, coconut sugar, vanilla, cinnamon, nutmeg and salt in a medium bowl. Then, whisk in almond milk.
2. Melt coconut oil or butter in a large skillet or on a griddle over medium heat.
3. Place bread slices into the egg mixture one by one and turn each one over to make sure the bread is well-coated.
4. Place bread slices in the skillet or on the griddle and cook until golden brown on each side – about 2 to 3 minutes.
5. Serve with pure maple syrup and fresh fruit if desired.

NUT-FREE GRANOLA

SERVES 6-8

PREP 5 minutes   COOK 30 minutes   TOTAL 35 minutes

⬤ NUT-FREE

This nut-free granola is extremely nutritious as it's packed with super-foods like hemp seeds, chia seeds and flaxseeds. Tahini is also blended with coconut oil and honey to create the crunchy yet nutritious texture. Dried fruits can be added once the granola is done cooking. Serve it with your favorite nondairy milk or yogurt or use it to top smoothies, yogurt or acai bowls.

INGREDIENTS

2 cups gluten-free rolled oats

¼ cup hemp seeds

¼ cup sesame seeds

¼ cup sunflower seeds

¼ cup unsweetened coconut flakes

2 tablespoons chia seeds

2 tablespoons flaxseeds

1 teaspoon ground cinnamon

½ teaspoon ground nutmeg

¼ teaspoon ground ginger

Pinch unrefined salt

¼ cup tahini

¼ cup coconut oil, softened or melted

¼ cup organic honey

OPTIONAL ADD-INS

Goji berries

Raisins

Dried apricots or figs, chopped

INSTRUCTIONS

1. Preheat oven to 300F and line a large baking sheet with parchment paper. Set aside.
2. Combine oats, hemp, sesame seeds, sunflower seeds, coconut flakes, chia seeds, flaxseeds, cinnamon, nutmeg, ginger and salt in a large mixing bowl. Stir well.
3. Blend tahini, coconut oil and honey in a blender until smooth, scraping down the sides with a spatula as needed.
4. Pour tahini mixture into dry granola mixture, and mix with your hands until well-combined.
5. Spread granola on the prepared baking sheet.
6. Bake for 35 minutes or until granola looks crisp, giving it a stir halfway through.
7. Allow to cool, toss in dried fruits if desired, and store in a large airtight container until ready to use.

APPLE CINNAMON OATMEAL

SERVES 1-2

PREP 2 minutes   COOK 8 minutes   TOTAL 10 minutes

Ⓝ NUT-FREE

There is nothing better than starting the day with a warm, cozy bowl of oatmeal on a wet, chilly day. Creamy oatmeal warms up the body and soothes the soul. It's also a great way to add fiber to the diet as well as minerals magnesium, iron and zinc. There is no added sugar as the apple, raisins and cinnamon add a natural touch of sweetness.

INGREDIENTS

1 cup water
Pinch unrefined salt
½ cup gluten-free rolled oats
¼ cup shredded apple
2 tablespoons unsulfured raisins
¼ teaspoon ground cinnamon
¼ cup coconut or almond milk

INSTRUCTIONS

1. Bring water to a boil in a small saucepan. Add a pinch of salt and stir in oats. Reduce heat to low, cover, and cook for about 3-4 minutes.
2. Stir in shredded apple, raisins and cinnamon.
3. Cover, and let simmer for another 2-3 minutes or until the oats have absorbed the water.
4. Turn off heat, add milk if you like, stir, and allow it to cool down for a few minutes before serving.
5. Pour oatmeal into a bowl and garnish with more cinnamon if you like.

OVERNIGHT CREAM OF OATS

SERVES 1

PREP 5 minutes   TOTAL 5 minutes plus chill time

(🥜) NUT-FREE

This is a breakfast that doesn't require any cooking. The oats soak overnight in milk and are blended in the morning until smooth. Then, they are tossed with flaxseeds, garnished with cinnamon and enjoyed at room temperature with any desired optional toppings. It's a nutritious and easy-to-eat meal, especially for little ones

INGREDIENTS

½ cup gluten-free rolled oats
½ cup almond, hemp or coconut milk
½ teaspoon flaxseeds
Pinch ground cinnamon

OPTIONAL TOPPINGS

Coconut flakes
Raw cacao nibs
Goji berries
Organic honey

INSTRUCTIONS

1. Put rolled oats and milk in a jar or bowl. Cover and refrigerate overnight.
2. In the morning, put in a smaller blender and blend until smooth.
3. Pour the oats into a bowl, add flaxseeds and stir, add any optional toppings if desired, add a little cinnamon to garnish and serve.

NOTE

If you don't like it cold, let the oats stand on the kitchen counter for several minutes or until it gets to room temperature before blending.

RASPBERRY BUCKWHEAT PANCAKES

SERVES 2

PREP 10 minutes   COOK 15 minutes   TOTAL 25 minutes

Ⓝ NUT-FREE

These gluten- and egg-free buckwheat pancakes are made with raspberries and cooked in coconut oil until slightly crisp. Buckwheat has a delicate, nutty flavor and pairs beautifully with raspberries. Add a drizzle of pure maple syrup, and you may fall in love with the combination of flavors.

INGREDIENTS

½ cup buckwheat flour
1 teaspoon ground flaxseeds
½ teaspoon baking powder
Pinch unrefined salt
½ cup raspberries, fresh or thawed from frozen
¾ cup nondairy milk
½ teaspoon vanilla extract
Coconut oil, for cooking
Additional raspberries, for garnish
Pure maple syrup, for serving

INSTRUCTIONS

1. Combine buckwheat flour, ground flaxseeds, baking powder and salt in a large mixing bowl.
2. Mash raspberries slightly in a medium mixing bowl. Add milk and vanilla, stir, and pour into the dry mix. Mix until well combined.
3. Rest dough for 5 minutes.
4. Add about 2 tablespoons of coconut oil to a large nonstick skillet or griddle over low heat. Using a ¼-cup measure, scoop the batter onto the warm skillet.
5. Cook pancakes until small bubbles form on the surface and the pancakes have started to change color, about 2 to 3 minutes. Then, flip over and cook for an additional 2 minutes or until they look crisp and slightly golden.
6. Repeat the process with the remaining batter, adding more coconut oil as needed.
7. Serve pancakes warm, and top with extra raspberries and pure maple syrup if desired.

TOFU SCRAMBLE

SERVES 2

PREP 10 minutes   COOK 10 minutes   TOTAL 20 minutes

Ⓝ NUT-FREE

If you want to try something different for breakfast or brunch, give this tofu scramble recipe a try. It's cooked with nutritional yeast, which is a deactivated yeast that gives a natural cheesy flavor while providing vitamin B12 and turmeric, a spice that has powerful anti-inflammatory properties and antioxidants. Serve the tofu with toast, avocado slices, halved tomatoes, sauerkraut or roasted potatoes for a complete breakfast.

INGREDIENTS

½ block organic firm or extra-firm tofu, drained

2 tablespoons nutritional yeast

½ teaspoon turmeric

¼ teaspoon red pepper flakes

¼ teaspoon unrefined salt, to taste

Freshly ground black pepper, to taste

2 tablespoons extra virgin olive oil or coconut oil

½ cup diced onions

1 clove garlic, minced

2 tablespoons vegetable broth or water

NOTE

Leftovers can be refrigerated and reheated the next day.

INSTRUCTIONS

1. With clean hands, press tofu between a kitchen towel or paper towel to remove excess water. Then, crumble tofu in small pieces and put into a medium mixing bowl.

2. Add nutritional yeast, turmeric, red pepper flakes, salt and black pepper to the crumbled tofu and mix well to coat the tofu.

3. Heat oil in a large skillet over medium heat. Sauté onions and garlic until soft and fragrant, about 2 minutes.

4. Add crumbled tofu mixture to the skillet and cook, stirring often, until tofu is hot throughout, about 8-10 minutes. Stir in broth or water.

5. When heated through, divide onto plates, and serve with your favorite side dishes.

SMOOTHIES

The smoothies you will find in the next few pages should please the whole family. They are colorful, flavorful, nutritious, and are made with a variety of fruits, vegetables, spices and superfoods. They are a great way to serve your children a variety of healthy—but still tasty—foods!

Salt is added in some of the recipes to balance flavors and provide minerals. You only use a few grains, and it should always be the unrefined kinds like Himalayan or Celtic salt. If you prefer not using, simply omit.

When using milk as a base, it's best to use homemade or store-bought, unsweetened milk. Smoothies are also best consumed on an empty stomach, so they make ideal breakfast or snack.

CHOCOLATE
HAZELNUT
SMOOTHIE

CREAMY
PEANUT
BUTTER
SMOOTHIE

RASPBERRY OAT
SMOOTHIE

CHOCOLATE HAZELNUT SMOOTHIE

SERVES 1

PREP 5 minutes   TOTAL 5 minutes

This smoothie, made with hazelnuts, cacao powder, vanilla and maple syrup, will remind you of the taste of Nutella™. Kids should enjoy this smoothie. If you have mesquite powder at home – a superfood that has a sweet caramel-like flavor – try adding a little hint of it. It makes the smoothie flavors pop. It's truly delicious.

INGREDIENTS

1¼ cup unsweetened coconut, almond or hazelnut milk
1 large ripe banana
⅓ cup roasted or raw hazelnuts or
1 tablespoon hazelnut butter
2 tablespoons raw cacao powder
1 tablespoon chia seeds
1-2 tablespoons pure maple syrup
¼ teaspoon nonalcoholic vanilla extract
Pinch Himalayan or Celtic salt
½ cup ice
½ teaspoon mesquite powder (optional)

INSTRUCTIONS

1. In a high-speed blender, add milk, banana, hazelnuts, cacao powder, chia seeds, maple syrup, vanilla, salt, ice and mesquite powder if using, and blend until smooth.

CREAMY PEANUT BUTTER SMOOTHIE

SERVES 1

PREP 5 minutes   TOTAL 5 minutes

This creamy peanut butter smoothie makes a nutritious breakfast or mid-morning snack. If you like the combination of peanut butter and chocolate, add a spoonful of raw cacao powder.

INGREDIENTS

1 cup almond or coconut milk
1 large frozen banana
2 tablespoons organic peanut butter
1 tablespoon chia seeds
1-2 tablespoons pure maple syrup or raw honey
¼ teaspoon ground cinnamon
Pinch Himalayan or Celtic salt
1 tablespoon raw cacao powder (optional)

INSTRUCTIONS

1. In a blender, add almond milk, banana, peanut butter, chia seeds, maple syrup, cinnamon and salt, and raw cacao powder if using, and blend until smooth.

RASPBERRY OAT SMOOTHIE

SERVES 1

PREP 5 minutes   TOTAL 5 minutes

If you like rich and creamy smoothies and love to enjoy them with a spoon, this smoothie is for you. Made with ingredients like oats, almond butter, chia seeds and coconut oil, this breakfast smoothie is packed with fiber, healthy fats and anti-oxidants that will sustain you until lunch.

INGREDIENTS

1¼ cup almond, coconut or hemp milk
½ cup gluten-free rolled oats
1 ripe banana
1 tablespoon almond butter
1 tablespoon chia seeds
1 tablespoon coconut oil
1 tablespoon raw honey or pure maple syrup
Pinch Himalayan or Celtic salt
1 cup frozen raspberries

INSTRUCTIONS

1. In a blender, add milk, oats, banana, almond butter, chia seeds, coconut oil, honey, salt and raspberries, and blend until nice and smooth.

BLUEBERRY PIE SMOOTHIE

SERVES 1

PREP 5 minutes   TOTAL 5 minutes

Inspired by the subtle flavors of blueberry pie, this creamy and nutritious smoothie is made with coconut milk, wild blueberries, almond butter, pure maple syrup, vanilla and cinnamon. Add rolled oats if you want a thicker, more substantial smoothie.

INGREDIENTS

1 cup coconut milk
1 medium ripe banana
1 cup frozen wild blueberries
1 tablespoon creamy almond butter
1 tablespoon pure maple syrup
¼ teaspoon nonalcoholic vanilla extract
Pinch ground cinnamon
¼ cup gluten-free rolled oats (optional)

INSTRUCTIONS

1. Put coconut milk in a blender along with the banana, blueberries, almond butter, maple syrup, vanilla and cinnamon, and oats if using, and blend until smooth.

COOKIE DOUGH SMOOTHIE

SERVES 1

PREP 5 minutes   TOTAL 5 minutes

Cookie dough for breakfast? Yes, please! This smoothie tastes like cookie dough minus the refined flour, sugar and oil. Your child will enjoy this smoothie, and you will love that your child is enjoying something healthy. It's a smoothie rich in minerals, antioxidants and healthy fats.

INGREDIENTS

1 cup almond milk
1 medium ripe banana
2 tablespoons raw cacao nibs
1 tablespoon chia seeds
1 tablespoon almond butter
2 Medjool dates, pitted
¼ teaspoon nonalcoholic vanilla
½ cup ice

INSTRUCTIONS

1. Put almond milk, banana, cacao nibs, chia seeds, almond butter, dates, vanilla and ice in your blender and blend until smooth.

HULK SMOOTHIE

SERVES 1

PREP 5 minutes   TOTAL 5 minutes

Ⓝ NUT-FREE

Green smoothies may not be very appealing for some children. However, with a name like "hulk smoothie" it may be more enjoyable for them. This smoothie has a delicate flavor and, although it's made with greens, you won't taste them – especially if using spinach. It's definitely a great first green smoothie.

INGREDIENTS

1½ cup almond milk
1 ripe banana
1 tablespoon hemp seeds
1 cup frozen mangoes
1 cup spinach or kale
1 tablespoon raw honey (optional)

INSTRUCTIONS

1. In a blender, put almond milk, banana, hemp seeds, mangoes, spinach or kale, and honey if using, and blend until smooth.

CARROT CAKE SMOOTHIE

SERVES 1

PREP 5 minutes   TOTAL 5 minutes

Carrot cake is one of my favorite cakes. I love the combination of flavors and textures, and the warm spices that make that cake so satisfying. This smoothie uses similar ingredients like carrots, raisins, pineapple, cinnamon and vanilla, and the almond butter makes it even richer and more fulfilling.

INGREDIENTS

1 cup coconut milk
1 medium ripe banana
1 medium carrot, chopped
1 cup frozen pineapple
2 tablespoons raisins
1 tablespoon almond butter
¼ teaspoon nonalcoholic vanilla extract
¼ teaspoon ground cinnamon
⅛ teaspoon ground ginger
Coconut flakes, for garnish (optional)

INSTRUCTIONS

1. In a high-speed blender, add coconut milk, banana, carrots, pineapple, raisins, almond butter, vanilla, cinnamon and ginger. Blend until smooth.
2. Garnish with coconut flakes if desired.

CARROT CAKE
SMOOTHIE

COOKIE DOUGH
SMOOTHIE

BLUEBERRY PIE
SMOOTHIE

DREAMY
STRAWBERRY
SMOOTHIE

GOLDEN MILK
SMOOTHIE

HULK
SMOOTHIE

DREAMY STRAWBERRY SMOOTHIE

SERVES 1

PREP 5 minutes   TOTAL 5 minutes

🥜 NUT-FREE

You will enjoy this velvety strawberry smoothie until the very last sip. It's rich, creamy, and so pretty. Do not skip the coconut oil as not only is it one of the ingredients that makes the smoothie so smooth, but it also provides healthy fats that will sustain you longer, improve energy and endurance and reduce sugar cravings.

INGREDIENTS

½ cup coconut milk
½ cup plain whole milk yogurt or coconut yogurt
1 small banana
1 cup frozen strawberries
1 tablespoon coconut oil
1 tablespoon raw honey

INSTRUCTIONS

1. In a blender, combine coconut milk, yogurt, banana, strawberries, coconut oil and honey, and blend until smooth.

GOLDEN MILK SMOOTHIE

SERVES 1

PREP 5 minutes   TOTAL 5 minutes

🥜 NUT-FREE

This anti-inflammatory smoothie is made with turmeric, cinnamon and ginger, but be reassured as the pungent taste of turmeric is balanced with the natural sweetness of the banana, mangoes and raw honey. The result is a creamy, nutritious and healing smoothie packed with vitamins, minerals, antioxidants and enzymes. Make sure not to skip the ground black pepper as it increases the absorption of turmeric.

INGREDIENTS

1 cup coconut milk
1 ripe banana
1 cup frozen mangoes
1 tablespoon raw honey
½ teaspoon ground turmeric
¼ teaspoon ground cinnamon
⅛ teaspoon ground ginger
Pinch ground black pepper

INSTRUCTIONS

1. In a blender, combine coconut milk, banana, mangoes, honey, turmeric, cinnamon, ginger and black pepper, and blend until smooth.

SOUPS AND STEWS

Soups and stews are nutritious, easy to digest and comforting. They are grounding and warming to the body and make an ideal meal during the cooler months of the year. Perfect for lunch or dinner or even as an appetizer, soups and stews are usually easy to make, are great as leftovers and freeze very well. They can be served on their own, with healthy bread, crackers or even with a crunchy salad or a colorful side dish.

In this chapter, you will find 10 different kinds of soups, both smooth and chunky, with different flavor profiles and ingredients. While chunky soups may not please every child, you may still want to give it a try as they are very nutritious and delicious. Otherwise, puréed soups are always a wonderful option as they are silky and satisfying and a great way to have your children eat their vegetables.

You will also find recipes for both chicken and vegetable broth in the wellness section at the end of the book. If you don't have homemade broth on hands, simply use a store-bought version, preferably one that is low in sodium. The amount of salt is based on the use of homemade or low-sodium broth.

AFRICAN PEANUT STEW

SERVES 4

PREP 10 minutes   COOK 30 minutes   TOTAL 40 minutes

Made with tomato paste, peanut butter, coconut milk, sweet potatoes and black beans, this vegan African-inspired stew is hearty, rich, flavorful and slightly spicy. It makes a very nourishing dinner on a chilly day. Serve the stew with brown rice, millet or cauliflower rice for a grain-free option and garnish with roasted peanuts and cilantro leaves.

INGREDIENTS

1 tablespoon coconut oil

1 large onion, diced

2 cloves garlic, minced

1 tablespoon freshly grated ginger

½ teaspoon ground coriander

¼ teaspoon red pepper flakes

1 can (6 ounces/170 grams) tomato paste

⅓ cup creamy peanut butter

1 large sweet potato, peeled and diced

1 can organic black beans, rinsed and drained

1 can (13.5 ounce/400 milliliters)
    full-fat coconut milk

1 cup water

1½ teaspoon unrefined salt

2 cups collard greens, kale or spinach,
    torn into 1-inch bites

½ lime, juiced

Cooked basmati rice, millet or
    cauliflower rice, to serve

Roasted peanuts, to garnish

Cilantro leaves, to garnish

INSTRUCTIONS

1. In a large pot, heat coconut oil over medium heat.
2. Add onions, garlic, and ginger and cook until onions are soft and fragrant, about 3 minutes.
3. Add coriander and red pepper flakes, stir, and cook for another minute.
4. Add tomato paste and peanut butter and mix well to combine.
5. Stir in sweet potato and black beans.
6. Add coconut milk, water and salt, and bring to a boil.
7. Reduce heat to low, cover partially, and simmer until sweet potatoes are tender, about 20-25 minutes, stirring frequently and scraping down the bottom of the pot.
8. Turn off heat. Stir in greens and lime juice.
9. Allow to cool and serve in bowls over cooked grains or cauliflower rice and garnish with roasted peanuts and cilantro leaves.

NOTE

You can substitute peanut butter with almond butter, and peanuts with roasted almonds. Do not garnish the stew with peanuts or almonds for babies due to the risk of choking.

FLOURLESS BEEF STEW

SERVES 4

PREP 25 minutes   COOK 2 hours, 15 minutes   TOTAL 2 hours, 40 minutes

⊛ NUT-FREE

Hearty and comforting, this beef stew is flourless and wine-free and adapted for small children or anyone avoiding grains, flour or alcohol. Stewed meat is very nourishing and a superb way to add iron into your child's diet. Although made in a Dutch oven on the stovetop, it can be made just as easily in the slow cooker. If you want a thick stew, thicken with arrowroot or tapioca starch. If you don't want to use potatoes, replace with turnips.

INGREDIENTS

2 tablespoons olive oil

2 pounds pastured beef stew meat or beef chuck, cut into bite-sized pieces

Unrefined salt

Freshly ground black pepper

1 tablespoon balsamic vinegar

1 large onion, chopped

2 cloves garlic, minced

½ teaspoon paprika

Dash ground allspice or ground cloves

1 bay leaf

1¼ teaspoon unrefined salt

¼ teaspoon ground black pepper

3 cups beef broth

1 pound organic baby potatoes, cut into halves

4 large carrots, chopped

3 ribs celery, chopped

2-3 tablespoons arrowroot or tapioca starch, to thicken (optional)

Fresh minced parsley, for serving (optional)

INSTRUCTIONS

FOR STOVETOP

1. If possible, remove meat from refrigerator and allow it to rest at room temperature for at least 30 minutes before cooking.
2. Season meat with salt and black pepper.
3. In a Dutch oven, heat olive oil over medium-high heat.
4. Sear meat in batches on all sides until browned. Remove meat and set aside. Repeat with remaining meat.
5. Add balsamic vinegar to deglaze pot and scrape bottom of pot with a wooden spatula.
6. Add onions and garlic, and cook until soft and fragrant, about 3 minutes.
7. If needed, deglaze the pot with a little broth, scraping the bottom of the pan as needed.
8. Add paprika, allspice, bay leaf, 1¼ teaspoon salt and ¼ teaspoon black pepper, and stir to coat all the onions.
9. Return meat to Dutch oven and stir.
10. Add broth and bring to a boil. Reduce heat to low, cover, and simmer for 90 minutes.
11. Add potatoes, carrots and celery, and cook until vegetables are tender, about 1 hour.
12. Discard bay leaf.
13. If desired, thicken the stew by combining thickener with 2 to 3 tablespoons of the broth in a small bowl to form a paste. Then, add to the stew and stir well. Heat for a few minutes to cook away the raw thickener taste.
14. Divide stew into bowls and garnish with minced parsley if desired.

FOR SLOW COOKER

1. Turn on your slow cooker.
2. Season meat with salt and black pepper and place meat in the slow cooker.
3. Add onions, garlic, carrots, celery and potatoes.
4. Add paprika, allspice, bay leaf, 1¼ teaspoon salt and ¼ teaspoon black pepper, and cover with broth.
5. Cook on low for 8 to 10 hours.
6. Remove bay leaf.
7. If desired, thicken the stew by combining thickener with 2 to 3 tablespoons of the broth in a small bowl to form a paste. Then, add to the stew and stir well. Heat for a few minutes to cook away the raw thickener taste.
8. Divide into bowls and garnish with minced parsley if desired.

POTATO LEEK SOUP

SERVES 4

PREP 5 minutes   COOK 30 minutes   TOTAL 35 minutes

Ⓝ NUT-FREE

Made with organic potatoes, fresh leeks and a hint of nutmeg, this dairy-free puréed soup is flavorful and satisfying. If you like, drizzle the soup with extra-virgin olive oil and garnish with sliced chives and freshly ground black pepper. For a more distinct flavor, garnish the soup with organic, crumbled turkey bacon.

INGREDIENTS

4 ¼ cup extra-virgin olive oil

1 medium onion, chopped

4 large leeks, white and pale green parts only, sliced (about 1 pound)

2 cloves garlic, minced

1 teaspoon unrefined salt

¼ teaspoon ground black pepper

¼ teaspoon ground nutmeg

1 bay leaf

1 pound organic russet potatoes, peeled and diced (about 2 medium potatoes)

6 cups chicken broth

OPTIONAL GARNISHES

Extra-virgin olive oil

Minced chives

Organic turkey bacon, cooked and crumbled

INSTRUCTIONS

1. In a large pot, heat olive oil over medium-low heat.
2. Add onions, leeks and garlic. Season with salt, black pepper and nutmeg, and cook, stirring often, until leeks have softened, about 10 minutes.
3. Add bay leaf and potatoes and cover with broth.
4. Bring to a boil, reduce heat to low, and simmer until potatoes are tender, about 15 to 20 minutes.
5. Discard bay leaf.
6. Transfer soup to a blender and blend carefully, in batches if necessary, until silky smooth.
7. Divide soup into bowls and add garnishes if desired.

NOTE

The soup tastes best made with chicken broth, but vegetable broth could be used for a vegetarian option.

EASY CHICKEN NOODLE SOUP

SERVES 4 to 6

PREP 15 minutes   COOK 1 hour, 15 minutes   TOTAL 1 hour, 30 minutes

NUT-FREE

Ah, chicken soup! The soup that warms up the body and nourishes the soul. This version is slightly different as it doesn't use a whole chicken but chicken breasts – preferably bone-in for more collagen and minerals – and gluten-free noodles. It's easy and quick to put together, making it perfect for the busy cook.

INGREDIENTS

2 tablespoons extra-virgin olive oil

1 medium yellow onion, diced

4 cloves garlic, minced

2 medium carrots, diced

4 celery stalks, diced

2 teaspoons dried parsley

½ teaspoon dried basil

¼ teaspoon dried thyme

1 bay leaf

1 tablespoon unrefined salt

Freshly ground black pepper

2 organic chicken breasts, preferably bone-in

10 cups water

2 cups gluten-free fusilli or noodles

NOTE

If you want a more traditional and healing soup, use homemade chicken bone broth.

INSTRUCTIONS

1. In a large pot, heat olive oil over medium-low heat. Add onions and garlic, and sauté until the onions are soft and fragrant, about 3 minutes.
2. Add carrots and celery, stir, and add parsley, basil, thyme, bay leaf, salt and black pepper. Stir again, and cook for another minute.
3. Add whole chicken breasts to the pot.
4. Cover with water and bring to a boil. Reduce heat to low, and simmer until the chicken is cooked through, about 45 to 60 minutes.
5. When chicken is done cooking, remove from pot. Use two forks to shred the chicken and set aside.
6. Bring water back to a boil. Add pasta, reduce heat to medium, and cook until pasta is al dente.
7. Turn off heat, add shredded chicken back to the pot, and serve.

CREAM OF BROCCOLI SOUP

SERVES 4

PREP 10 minutes   COOK 25 minutes   TOTAL 35 minutes

Ⓝ NUT-FREE

A classic and favorite of many children, this healthy version is dairy-free and made with coconut milk. The result is a creamy, nourishing and satisfying soup. You can serve it all year long and it is wonderful served with a good quality, warm bread.

INGREDIENTS

1 tablespoon extra-virgin olive oil

1 large onion, chopped

2 cloves garlic, minced

2 stalks celery, chopped

1 teaspoon unrefined salt

¼ teaspoon ground black pepper

¼ teaspoon dried thyme

1 medium russet potato, peeled and chopped

1 large broccoli, cut into florets and stems peeled and chopped

3 cups chicken broth

1 can (13.5 ounces/400 milliliters) full-fat coconut milk

INSTRUCTIONS

1. In a large pot, heat olive oil over medium-low heat.
2. Add onions and garlic, stir and cook until soft and fragrant, about 3 minutes.
3. Add celery, salt, black pepper and thyme, stir, and cook for another minute.
4. Add potatoes and broccoli to the pot.
5. Cover with broth. Bring to a boil, reduce heat to low, cover, and simmer until potatoes are tender, about 15 to 20 minutes.
6. Transfer soup to a blender, in batches if necessary, and blend carefully until smooth.
7. Transfer soup back to the pot and stir in coconut milk.
8. Divide soup into bowls and serve.

MINESTRONE WITH QUINOA AND KALE

SERVES 8

PREP 15 minutes   COOK 30 minutes   TOTAL 45 minutes

Ⓝ NUT-FREE

This chunky Italian minestrone is made with sweet potatoes, peas, quinoa, beans and kale. It's nutritious, flavorful and easy to make. Even if you don't like chunky soup, give it a try. You may enjoy this one! To enhance umami flavor, garnish the soup with freshly grated Parmesan cheese if you like.

INGREDIENTS

2 tablespoons extra-virgin olive oil
1 large onion, diced
4 cloves garlic, minced
2 large carrots, diced
2 stalks celery, diced
1 tablespoon unrefined salt
¼ teaspoon ground black pepper
1 teaspoon dried oregano
1 bay leaf
1 small sweet potato, peeled and
    diced (about 1 cup)
¾ cup peas, fresh or frozen
1 can (15 ounces/425 grams) kidney
    beans, rinsed and drained
1 can (15 ounces/425 grams) cannellini
    beans, rinsed and drained
1 can (14.5 ounces/ 411 grams) diced tomatoes
8-10 cups low-sodium vegetable broth
¾ cup quinoa, rinsed and drained
1 cup kale, stemmed and torn into small pieces
1 tablespoon fresh lemon juice
1 tablespoon minced parsley
Freshly grated Parmesan cheese,
    to serve (optional)

INSTRUCTIONS

1. In a large pot, heat olive oil over medium heat.
2. Add onions and garlic, and cook about 3 minutes, until soft and fragrant.
3. Add carrots and celery, along with the salt, black pepper, oregano and bay leaf. Cook for 2 minutes, stirring often.
4. Add sweet potatoes, peas and beans and stir again.
5. Add tomatoes, stir and cover with broth. Bring to a boil, then add quinoa. Reduce heat to low, cover, and simmer until potatoes are tender and quinoa is cooked, about 20 minutes.
6. Turn off heat. Stir in lemon juice and minced parsley.
7. Divide soup into bowls and garnish with fresh Parmesan cheese if you like.

YELLOW SPLIT PEA SOUP

SERVES 6

PREP 15 minutes   COOK 3 hours   TOTAL 3 hours, 15 minutes

Ⓝ NUT-FREE

Growing up in Quebec, traditional split pea soup was often on the menu, especially during the cold months of the year. This version is vegetarian and made with thyme, smoked paprika and nutritional yeast, which gives the soup a light, smoky flavor while enhancing umami flavor, also known as the fifth taste. The soup is thick, hearty and flavorful and is delicious served with avocado toast or a piece of crusty French bread.

INGREDIENTS

2 tablespoons extra-virgin olive oil
1 large yellow onion, diced
4 cloves garlic, minced
3 stalks celery, diced
2 medium carrots, diced
1 teaspoon dried thyme or 1 tablespoon fresh thyme leaves
1 teaspoon smoked paprika
1 bay leaf
¼ teaspoon ground black pepper
2 cups dry yellow split peas, rinsed
¼ cup nutritional yeast
8 cups low-sodium vegetable broth
1½ teaspoon unrefined salt
Minced parsley, for garnish (optional)

INSTRUCTIONS

1. In a Dutch oven or large pot, heat olive oil over medium heat.
2. Add onions, garlic, celery and carrots, and cook, stirring frequently, until onions have softened, about 8 minutes.
3. Stir in thyme, paprika, bay leaf and black pepper, and cook for another 2 to 5 minutes.
4. Add peas and nutritional yeast and stir to combine.
5. Add vegetable broth. Bring to a boil, reduce heat to low, cover, and let simmer, stirring occasionally, until peas are tender, about 2 to 3 hours.
6. Discard bay leaf and stir in salt.
7. Allow to cool before serving and garnish with parsley if desired.

NOTES

- Split peas don't require soaking but need to be rinsed prior to cooking.
- Soup can be frozen for up to 3 months.

RED LENTIL COCONUT DHAL

SERVES 6

PREP 10 minutes   COOK 25 minutes   TOTAL 35 minutes

🥜 NUT-FREE

One of my favorite Indian meals, this vegetarian dhal is made with red lentils, curry, cumin, turmeric, red pepper flakes and coconut milk. It's creamy, fragrant, nutritious and utterly delicious. It's also very easy to create and makes wonderful leftovers. Serve the dhal with basmati rice or naan bread and garnish with cilantro, if you like.

INGREDIENTS

2 tablespoons coconut oil or ghee
1 large onion, diced
2 garlic cloves, minced
1 tablespoon freshly grated ginger
1 tablespoon curry powder
2 teaspoon ground cumin
¼ teaspoon ground turmeric
Pinch red pepper flakes
2 teaspoon unrefined salt
Freshly ground black pepper
2 cups red lentils, rinsed
2 cups water
1 can (13.5 ounces/400 milliliters)
    full-fat coconut milk
½ lemon, juiced

Cooked basmati rice or naan bread, for serving
Minced cilantro, to garnish

INSTRUCTIONS

1. In a large pot, heat coconut oil over medium heat.
2. Add onion, garlic and ginger, and cook until onions are soft and fragrant, about 3 minutes.
3. Add curry, cumin, turmeric, red pepper flakes, salt and black pepper, and stir to coat all the onion mixture.
4. Add lentils and stir to combine. Cover with water.
5. Bring to a boil, reduce heat to low, cover, and simmer until lentils are cooked, about 20 minutes. Stir occasionally to avoid having dhal stick at the bottom of the pan.
6. Turn off heat. Stir in coconut milk and lemon juice.
7. Serve over basmati rice or with naan bread, and garnish with cilantro if desired.

NOTE

To boost nutrient intake, try adding a handful of spinach or kale at the end of cooking.

ROASTED BUTTERNUT SQUASH SOUP

SERVES 4

PREP 10 minutes   COOK 1 hour, 10 minutes   TOTAL 1 hour, 20 minutes

Ⓝ NUT-FREE

One of my favorite soups, this roasted butternut squash is sweet and creamy while being creamless. The squash is first roasted until caramelized before being simmered on the stovetop with nutmeg, red pepper flakes and chicken broth. It's then puréed with coconut milk and pure maple syrup until smooth and silky. The soup is lovely garnished with toasted squash or pumpkin seeds or served with artisanal, rustic bread.

INGREDIENTS

1 large butternut squash, about 4 pounds
2 tablespoons extra-virgin olive oil, divided
1 large onion, chopped
4 cloves garlic, minced
1½ teaspoon unrefined salt
¾ teaspoon ground nutmeg
Pinch red pepper flakes

3 cups low-sodium chicken broth
1 can (13.5 ounces/400 milliliters)
    full-fat coconut milk
1 tablespoon pure maple syrup
Toasted squash or pumpkin seeds,
    for garnish (optional)

INSTRUCTIONS

1. Preheat oven to 400F.
2. Cut squash in half lengthwise. Scoop out and discard seeds and stringy flesh. Put squash cut-side down onto a large baking sheet. Roast until fork tender, about 40 minutes. Allow squash to cool slightly before peeling the skin off and scooping out the flesh.
3. When squash is almost done cooking, add olive oil to a large pot along with the onions and garlic. Cook on medium heat, stirring often, until onions are soft and start to caramelize, about 10 minutes. Deglaze pan as needed with chicken broth.
4. Season with salt, nutmeg and red pepper flakes, and stir to combine.
5. Add squash to the pot and stir in broth. Bring to a boil then reduce heat to low, cover, and cook for 15 to 20 minutes.

6. Turn off heat and allow to cool for a few minutes.
7. Transfer soup to a blender and blend carefully, in batches if necessary, until smooth and silky.
8. Return soup back to pot and stir in coconut milk and maple syrup.
9. Divide soup into bowls and garnish with toasted squash or pumpkin seeds, if desired.

NOTE

To toast squash or pumpkin seeds, put the seeds in a skillet, drizzle with olive oil – enough to coat all the seeds – sprinkle with unrefined salt, and cook on medium heat for a minute or two until they start to change color and get slightly puffed.

VEGETARIAN CHILI

PREP 20 minutes   COOK 50 minutes   TOTAL 1 hour, 10 minutes

Ⓝ NUT-FREE

This crowd-pleasing vegetarian chili is savory, nutritious and colorful. It's made with three different types of beans as well as fresh corn. It's pretty mild, which means it is usually more appreciated by children. Garnish with diced avocado and cilantro and serve with homemade cornbread or tortilla chips if desired.

INGREDIENTS

2 tablespoons extra-virgin olive oil

1 large onion, diced

2 cloves garlic, minced

1 small jalapeño, seeded and minced

1 green bell pepper, seeded and diced

2 tablespoons chili powder

1 tablespoon ground cumin

½ tablespoon dried oregano

1 teaspoon ground coriander

2 teaspoons unrefined salt

1 can (28 ounces/793 grams) diced
    tomatoes, preferably fire-roasted

1 can (15 ounces/425 grams) pinto
    beans, rinsed and drained

1 can (15 ounces/425 grams) black
    beans, rinsed and drained

1 can (15 ounces/425 grams) black-
    eyed peas, rinsed and drained

4 ears fresh corn, husked (about 2 cups)

1 cup water

OPTIONAL GARNISHES

Diced avocado

Minced cilantro

Lime wedges

INSTRUCTIONS

1. Heat olive oil over medium heat. Add onions and sauté until soft and fragrant, about 3 minutes. Add garlic and jalapeno, stir, and sauté for another 2 minutes.

2. Add bell pepper, chili powder, cumin, oregano, coriander and salt, stir, and cook for another minute.

3. Add tomatoes, beans, corn and water.

4. Bring to a boil, reduce heat to low, cover partially, and simmer for 40 minutes.

5. Turn off heat, divide between bowls, and garnish with diced avocado, fresh cilantro, and lime wedges if desired.

NOTE

If you have kale lovers in your family, try adding a cup of chopped kale to the chili at the end of cooking.

SALADS

Perfect for picnics, potlucks or a lunch box, salads make refreshing, nutritious and flavorful meals or side dishes. Usually made with raw ingredients, they are full of vitamins, minerals, fibers, enzymes and phytonutrients. Salads are very versatile so that you can easily adjust the ingredients to your family's liking. They are also pleasant to eat as they can contain a variety of colors, textures and flavors.

If you have little ones at home, you may want to cut vegetables into smaller, bite-sized pieces and avoid serving them nuts, seeds and dried fruits that can be too hard or chewy. However, chia, flax, hemp and sesame seeds are suitable. It's important to offer and encourage your children to eat fresh vegetables and fruits daily and as early as possible so they can develop a taste for them as well as develop good eating habits.

The dressings are flavorful and easy to make. You can whisk, blend or shake them in a jar and even prepare them in advance. I highly recommend using high-quality ingredients as it impacts the taste and nutritional value of the dressings. If possible, use unrefined, cold-pressed oils; fresh lemons for lemon juice; and organic, local honey or pure maple syrup for sweetness.

For the busy cook at home, take a day during the week to make a dressing, cook beans or grains or to make a large salad and store it in individual containers. If the salad contains avocado, eat within the same day or add when serving. Dressing can be made in larger quantities for the week then stored in a small, separate jar.

WHITE BEAN TUNA SALAD

SERVES 2

PREP 10 minutes   TOTAL 10 minutes

Ⓝ NUT-FREE

Made with chunk light tuna and white cannellini beans, this salad is high in protein and fiber. It also contains diced avocado, red bell pepper and celery. Serve it on its own, as a side dish or with a piece of country bread.

INGREDIENTS

SALAD

1 can (5 ounces/142 grams) wild-caught chunk light tuna (skipjack or tongol), drained and flaked
1 cup cooked cannellini beans
1 avocado, pitted and chopped
¼ cup diced red bell pepper
1 stalk celery, diced
1 tablespoon minced parsley

VINAIGRETTE

2 tablespoons fresh lemon juice
½ teaspoon unrefined salt
Freshly ground black pepper
3 tablespoons extra-virgin olive oil

INSTRUCTIONS

1. Combine tuna, beans, avocado, red bell pepper, celery and parsley in a large mixing bowl.
2. Combine lemon juice with salt and black pepper in a small bowl. Whisk in olive oil and add dressing to salad. Stir to combine.
3. Eat immediately or refrigerate until ready to serve.

CHICKEN WALDORF SALAD

SERVES 2-4

PREP 15 minutes   TOTAL 15 minutes

Ⓝ NUT-FREE

This Waldorf salad is made with red grapes, green apples, celery and red onions and tossed in a refreshing yogurt sauce. Use boiled or rotisserie chicken and white or dark meat – or both! If not serving to little ones, you may want to add walnuts and cut chicken, fruits and vegetables into larger pieces.

INGREDIENTS

SALAD

2 cups cooked chicken, shredded or diced
½ cup diced red grapes, quartered
½ green apple, diced
1 stalk celery, diced
2 tablespoons finely diced red onions
¼ cup chopped walnuts (optional)

YOGURT DRESSING

¼ cup organic plain full-fat or Greek yogurt
2 tablespoons fresh lemon juice
1 teaspoon organic honey or pure maple syrup
½ teaspoon unrefined salt
Freshly ground black pepper

INSTRUCTIONS

1. Put chicken, grapes, apple, celery, onions and walnuts if using in a medium mixing bowl.
2. Make dressing by whisking yogurt, lemon juice, honey, salt and black pepper in a small bowl until well combined.
3. Toss salad with dressing and serve immediately or refrigerate until ready to use.

NOTES

- For a dairy-free option, substitute with plain almond or coconut yogurt.
- For a richer sauce, add 1 to 2 more tablespoons of yogurt.

CHICKPEA SALAD WITH LEMON OREGANO VINAIGRETTE

SERVES 4

PREP 15 minutes   TOTAL 15 minutes

Ⓝ NUT-FREE

Inspired by Mediterranean flavors, this chickpea salad is made with Roma tomatoes, Persian cucumbers, red onions and avocado. Feta cheese is optional but a terrific addition if your family likes it. Great to enjoy during the summer, this salad makes a wonderful side dish or light meal. You can also serve it with pita bread and hummus or grilled chicken.

INGREDIENTS

SALAD

1 can (15 ounces/425 grams) chickpeas, drained and rinsed

2 Roma tomatoes, diced

2 Persian cucumbers, diced

1 small yellow bell pepper, diced

½ cup diced red onions

8 Kalamata olives, pitted and halved

1 avocado, pitted and chopped

¼ cup minced parsley

½ cup crumbled feta cheese (optional)

LEMON OREGANO VINAIGRETTE

2 tablespoons fresh lemon juice

1 teaspoon dried oregano

½ teaspoon Dijon mustard

½ teaspoon unrefined salt

½ teaspoon ground black pepper

¼ cup extra-virgin olive oil

INSTRUCTIONS

1. Combine chickpeas, tomatoes, cucumbers, red onions, avocado, parsley and feta cheese if using in a large mixing bowl.
2. Whisk lemon juice, oregano, mustard, salt and black pepper together. Add olive oil slowly until combined.
3. Add dressing to salad, stir, and enjoy immediately or refrigerate until ready to eat.

COLESLAW WITH APPLES AND POPPY SEEDS

SERVES 6

PREP 20 minutes   TOTAL 20 minutes

(Ⓝ) NUT-FREE

Deliciously nutritious, this colorful and creamy slaw makes a perfect side dish for sandwiches, burgers, vegetarian patties, grilled meat, fish or tofu. It's also a lovely salad to bring to potlucks and picnics.

INGREDIENTS

½ head red cabbage, outer leaf removed
½ head green cabbage, outer leaf removed
2 large carrots, tops trimmed
1 apple, such as Gala or Fuji, cored
1 tablespoon poppy seeds

DRESSING

½ cup extra-virgin olive oil
¼ cup unpasteurized apple cider vinegar
1 tablespoon Dijon mustard
1 tablespoon raw honey or pure maple syrup
1½ teaspoon unrefined salt
¾ teaspoon ground black pepper

INSTRUCTIONS

1. With the help of a food processor, mandolin or box grater, slice cabbage, carrots and apple thinly. Then, put into a large mixing bowl and stir in poppy seeds.
2. Massage the salad with clean hands to soften the cabbage, about 1 minute.
3. In a small blender, place olive oil, apple cider vinegar, mustard, honey, salt and black pepper and blend until smooth.
4. Pour dressing in the salad, stir well and serve at room temperature or refrigerate until ready to use.

MEXICAN BEAN SALAD WITH CHILI LIME VINAIGRETTE

SERVES 6

PREP 25 minutes   TOTAL 25 minutes

Ⓝ NUT-FREE

This salad is a combination of three types of beans, fresh corn, tomatoes, bell peppers, red onions and cilantro and is tossed in a chili lime vinaigrette. It's colorful, festive and very flavorful. It's a great salad to make for parties, potlucks and picnics or as a beautiful side dish. Although delicious eaten immediately, the salad tastes even better when made ahead as it allows the flavors to marinate. Serve chilled or at room temperature.

INGREDIENTS

SALAD

1 can (15 ounces/425 grams) can pinto peas, rinsed and drained

1 can (15 ounces/425 grams) can black-eyed peas, rinsed and drained

1 can (15 ounces/425 grams) can black beans, rinsed and drained

2 ears fresh corn kernels, cut off the cob (about 1½ cups)

1 large Roma tomato, chopped

1 green bell pepper, diced

1 small red onion, finely diced (about 1 cup)

⅓ cup minced cilantro

1 large avocado, pitted and chopped

CHILI LIME VINAIGRETTE

1 lime, juiced (about ¼ cup)

1 teaspoon local honey or pure maple syrup

1 teaspoon chili powder

½ teaspoon ground cumin

1¼ teaspoon unrefined salt

⅓ cup extra-virgin olive oil

INSTRUCTIONS

1. Combine beans, corn kernels, tomatoes, bell pepper, red onion and cilantro in a large mixing bowl. If serving immediately, add avocado. Otherwise, add avocado when serving.
2. Make the dressing by whisking lime juice, honey, chili, cumin and salt in a small bowl. Then, whisk in olive oil slowly until well combined.
3. Pour dressing onto salad and toss to combine.
4. Serve or refrigerate until ready to use.

NOTE

Corn is a grain and a common allergen. Babies may also have difficulty to digest it. Wait until your child is at least one year old to serve corn. If your family doesn't eat corn, simply omit or replace with cooked quinoa instead.

KALE SALAD WITH MAPLE BALSAMIC DRESSING

SERVES 4-6

PREP 20 minutes   TOTAL 20 minutes

Ⓝ NUT-FREE

The secret to making a palatable, tender kale salad is to massage the leaves until they start to soften and wilt. Add additional ingredients to make the salad even tastier, then complete by tossing it with a delectable dressing like this creamy maple balsamic dressing. The result is a soft, velvety and scrumptious kale salad that should please the whole family.

INGREDIENTS

1 large bunch curly kale, stemmed and torn into small pieces (about 12 cups)

1 apple, peeled, cored and thinly sliced

1 avocado, pitted and chopped

¼ cup organic dried cranberries, preferably unsweetened

¼ cup pumpkin seeds or 2 tablespoons hemp seeds

MAPLE BALSAMIC DRESSING

2 tablespoons balsamic vinegar

1 tablespoon pure maple syrup

½ teaspoon Dijon mustard

1 small clove garlic, minced

½ teaspoon unrefined salt

Freshly ground black pepper

¼ cup extra-virgin olive oil

INSTRUCTIONS

1. Wash and dry the kale, and then transfer to a large mixing bowl.
2. Sprinkle leaves with salt and, with clean hands, massage the kale until the leaves start to soften and wilt, about 2 minutes.
3. Add apple slices, avocado, cranberries and pumpkin seeds or hemp seeds and combine well.
4. Make the dressing by whisking the balsamic vinegar, maple syrup, Dijon mustard, garlic, salt and black pepper in a small bowl. Then, whisk in olive oil slowly until well combined.
5. Add dressing to the salad and toss to combine.
6. Serve immediately or refrigerate until ready to use.

NOTE

The salad is also very delicious with avocado and hemp seeds only. It is more simple but just as delightful. If you dislike cranberries, try it with fresh sliced strawberries instead.

QUINOA SALAD

SERVES 4-6

PREP 10 minutes   COOK 20 minutes   TOTAL 30 minutes

Ⓝ NUT-FREE

Light and nutritious, this is a great first quinoa salad for little ones. The vegetables are cut into small pieces, and the herbs are minced finely. Quinoa is a complete source of protein while being gluten-free. For extra protein, add chickpeas. For extra crunchiness, add walnuts, unless serving to babies and toddlers. Cook the quinoa ahead of time so that it has time to cool down before assembling the salad.

INGREDIENTS

SALAD

1 cup dry quinoa, rinsed
2 cups water
Pinch unrefined salt
1 Persian cucumber, diced
1 Roma tomato, diced
1 carrot, peeled and shredded
1 large avocado, pitted and chopped
1 tablespoon minced parsley
1 tablespoon minced mint
¼ cup finely diced red onions
1 can (15 ounces/425 grams) chickpeas, rinsed and drained (optional)
¼ cup chopped walnuts (optional)

DRESSING

2 tablespoons fresh lemon juice
½ teaspoon Dijon mustard
½ teaspoon unrefined salt
Freshly ground black pepper
¼ cup extra-virgin olive oil

INSTRUCTIONS

1. Put quinoa into a fine-mesh strainer and rinse under cold running water. Drain.
2. Bring water to a boil in a small saucepan. Add quinoa and a pinch of salt, stir, reduce heat to low, cover, and cook until the quinoa is softened and the water has been absorbed, about 15 minutes. Turn off heat, allow the quinoa to rest for 5 minutes and fluff gently with a fork. Transfer to a bowl and refrigerate until ready to use.
3. Whisk together lemon juice, Dijon mustard, salt and black pepper in a small bowl, and whisk in olive oil gradually. Set aside.
4. When cooled down, add quinoa to a large mixing bowl. Stir in cucumbers, tomatoes, carrots, avocados, parsley and chickpeas if using.
5. Add the salad dressing and mix well. Enjoy immediately or refrigerate until ready to eat.

NOTE

Make sure to rinse the quinoa under running water prior to cooking.
This important step removes the saponins that make the quinoa slightly bitter.

RAINBOW PASTA SALAD

SERVES 4-6

PREP 15 minutes   COOK 15 minutes   TOTAL 30 minutes

🥜 NUT-FREE

This is a beautiful pasta salad filled with colors, textures and flavors. Use your favorite healthy pasta and cut vegetables into tiny pieces. The dressing is light and flavorful. Overall, it's a refreshing, light and nutritious pasta salad — perfect for summer!

INGREDIENTS

SALAD

1 package (16 ounces/454 grams) gluten-free elbow pasta (or your favorite pasta)
¾ cup frozen corn kernels (or fresh from 1 ear of corn)
¾ cup frozen garden peas
½ red bell pepper, finely diced
1 radish, thinly sliced
1 small carrot, peeled and finely diced (about ¼ cup)
⅓ cup finely diced tomatoes
⅓ cup small broccoli florets
⅓ cup finely diced red onions
1 tablespoon minced parsley

MAPLE OREGANO DRESSING

1 lemon, juiced
2 tablespoons pure maple syrup
1 small clove garlic, peeled and minced
½ teaspoon Dijon mustard
1 teaspoon dried oregano
1 teaspoon unrefined salt
¼ teaspoon red pepper flakes
½ cup extra-virgin olive oil

INSTRUCTIONS

1. Cook pasta in salted boiling water according to package directions. Stir in frozen corn and peas about 2 to 3 minutes before pasta is done cooking. Drain in a colander and return to pot.

2. While pasta is cooking, make the herb dressing. Whisk together lemon juice, apple cider vinegar, maple syrup, garlic, mustard, basil, oregano, salt and red pepper flakes in a small bowl, and whisk in olive oil slowly until emulsified or blend all ingredients in a blender until smooth. Set aside.

3. Add bell peppers, radishes, carrots, tomatoes, broccoli, red onions and parsley to pasta.

4. Stir in dressing and toss to combine. Refrigerate and chill for 1 hour before serving.

AVOCADO EGG SALAD

SERVES 2-4

PREP 4 minutes   COOK 6 minutes   TOTAL 10 minutes

Ⓝ NUT-FREE

Egg salad is a classic sandwich filling enjoyed by many people. Instead of being made with mayonnaise, this recipe uses extra-virgin olive oil, fresh lemon juice and avocado. It's healthy, satisfying and nutritious. Try it between two slices of bread or as an open-faced sandwich. For adults, try adding a scoop on top of a green salad. The salad is best eaten the same day.

INGREDIENTS

4 pastured eggs
1 medium ripe avocado, pitted and chopped
1 tablespoon extra-virgin olive oil
1 tablespoon fresh lemon juice
¼ teaspoon unrefined salt
Freshly ground black pepper
Pinch paprika
1 small celery stalk, finely diced (optional)

INSTRUCTIONS

1. Place eggs in a pot and cover with cold water. Bring to a boil, cover, remove from heat and set aside for 8 minutes. Drain eggs and cool in cold water.
2. Peel and chop the eggs coarsely, then put them into a medium mixing bowl and mash with a fork or potato masher.
3. Add avocado, olive oil, lemon juice, salt, black pepper, paprika and celery if using, and mix until well combined.
4. Serve immediately or refrigerate until ready to eat.

TUNA CUCUMBER AVOCADO SALAD

SERVES 2

PREP 10 minutes   TOTAL 10 minutes

⊛ NUT-FREE

This nutritious salad is light and colorful and lovely eaten on its own or with a piece of artisanal bread. The salad is best eaten immediately or within the same day of making it.

INGREDIENTS

SALAD

1 can (5 ounces/142 grams) wild-caught chunk light tuna
(skipjack or tongol), drained and flaked
1 medium ripe avocado, pitted and chopped
1 cup diced cucumbers
(from about 1 Persian cucumber or ⅓ English cucumber)
½ cup diced red bell pepper
¼ cup finely diced red onion
1 tablespoon minced cilantro

DRESSING

1 tablespoon extra-virgin olive oil
1 tablespoon fresh lemon juice
¼ teaspoon unrefined salt
Freshly ground black pepper

INSTRUCTIONS

1. Combine tuna, avocado, cucumbers, red bell peppers, red onions and cilantro in a large bowl.
2. Add olive oil, lemon juice, salt and black pepper, and stir to combine.
3. Eat immediately or refrigerate in an airtight container.

WILD RICE SALAD WITH MAPLE CIDER DRESSING

SERVES 4-6

PREP 15 minutes   COOK 45 minutes   TOTAL 1 hour

Wild rice is not a grain but an aquatic grass that is native to North America. It's gluten-free, alkaline-forming, rich in antioxidants and a good source of protein. This salad is a combination of wild rice, apples, dried cranberries and chopped walnuts and is tossed in a maple cider dressing. If you'd like, add crumbled goat cheese. This salad is perfect for autumn.

INGREDIENTS

SALAD

1 cup wild rice

3 cups water

Pinch unrefined salt

1 local or red apple, peeled and diced

¼ cup dried cranberries

¼ cup chopped walnuts

2 tablespoons minced parsley

Crumbled goat cheese (optional)

MAPLE CIDER DRESSING

2 tablespoons apple cider vinegar

2 tablespoons pure maple syrup

½ teaspoon Dijon mustard

1 small garlic clove, peeled and minced

1 teaspoon unrefined salt

⅛ teaspoon cayenne pepper

¼ cup extra-virgin olive oil

INSTRUCTIONS

1. Bring water to a boil in a medium saucepan. Add a pinch of salt, stir in rice, cover, reduce heat to low, and simmer for 40 minutes. Turn off heat, fluff rice with a fork, allow to cool, and store in the refrigerator.

2. Whisk cider vinegar, maple syrup, mustard, garlic, salt and cayenne pepper in a small bowl. Whisk in olive oil gradually until emulsified. Set aside.

3. When rice has cooled down, transfer to a large mixing bowl. Add apples, cranberries, walnuts, parsley and goat cheese if using and toss with vinaigrette.

4. Serve immediately or refrigerate until ready to eat.

EGGS

Eggs are one of the most nutrient-dense foods available. They make an ideal food for growing children and teenagers as well as pregnant and breastfeeding women. Not only they are a complete protein food, but they are also a rich source of vitamins A, D and E as well as vitamin B12, folate, choline, iron, zinc and selenium. Eggs support healthy growth and repair, immune function, eyesight and brain development. They are one of nature's most perfect foods.

Pastured eggs from a local farmer are the healthiest choice because the hens are allowed to roam free on open pastures, eating bugs and grass and are exposed to sun and fresh air. Therefore, they tend to produce more nutritious eggs. If your local grocery store doesn't carry them, ask them to do so. You may also find them at your farmers' market or from a local farmer. They may even come in a variety of shell colors and sizes.

If you have an infant at home, and you suspect or are concerned about an egg allergy, start by giving the yolk only as most people who are allergic to eggs react to the proteins found in the white. It's also now known that introducing whole eggs early in a child's diet can reduce their chances of developing an egg allergy. Avoid cooking eggs at high temperatures or overcooking them. Try them with avocado, vegetables or sweet potatoes.

BAKED EGG WITH SWEET POTATO AND SPINACH

SERVES 2-4

PREP 25 minutes   COOK 20 minutes   TOTAL 45 minutes

Ⓝ NUT-FREE

Deliciously nutritious, this dish is made with pastured eggs, mashed sweet potatoes and wilted spinach – three known superfoods. Bake them individually in ramekins and serve them with a side of multigrain toasts, roasted vegetables or a garden salad for a more complete meal. They are best eaten immediately. Serve one per child or two per adult.

INGREDIENTS

1 pound sweet potato, peeled and diced (about 2 medium)
1 teaspoon extra-virgin olive oil
3 cups spinach

4 pastured eggs
Unrefined salt, to taste
Freshly ground black pepper, to taste
Paprika, to taste

INSTRUCTIONS

1. Preheat oven to 400F and oil ramekins lightly with olive oil. Place ramekins on a baking sheet.
2. Bring a medium pot of water to a boil. Season with salt and add sweet potatoes. Boil until potatoes are tender, about 8 to 10 minutes. Drain in a colander.
3. Put sweet potatoes in a food processor, drizzle with a teaspoon of olive oil, add a pinch of salt and process until smooth and silky. If you don't have a food processor, put potatoes back to the pot and mash with a potato masher until smooth. Reserve.
4. Place spinach in a medium pot of boiling water and cook until wilted, about 1 to 2 minutes. Drain in a colander. Reserve.
5. Divide potato purée between ramekins.
6. Remove excess water from spinach and add to the ramekins on top of each sweet potato layer.
7. One at the time, break eggs into ramekins carefully onto the spinach layer and season with salt, black pepper and paprika.
8. Put the baking sheet with the ramekins in the oven and bake until eggs are set and whites have solidified, about 18 to 20 minutes.
9. Remove ramekins from oven and allow to cool for a few minutes before serving.

NOTE

If you prefer, substitute spinach for kale.

BAKED SPANISH TORTILLA WITH KALE

SERVES 6

PREP 10 minutes   COOK 35 minutes   TOTAL 45 minutes

Ⓝ NUT-FREE

This version of the classic Spanish tortilla uses organic sliced potatoes, thinly sliced onions and chopped kale and is baked in the oven until cooked and slightly golden brown. This crowd-pleasing dish is lovely served with a green salad for a refreshing, light summer meal.

INGREDIENTS

3 tablespoons extra-virgin olive oil, divided
1 small onion, thinly sliced
2 cups stemmed and chopped kale
1 pound organic white potatoes, peeled and thinly sliced
(about 1 large or 3 or 4 medium)
8 pastured eggs
1 teaspoon unrefined salt
¼ teaspoon ground black pepper

INSTRUCTIONS

1. Preheat oven to 400F.
2. Heat 1 tablespoon olive oil over medium heat in a large oven-proof skillet. Add onions and cook until very soft and translucent, about 5 minutes.
3. Add kale and cook until softened, about 2 minutes. Transfer vegetables to a bowl and set aside.
4. Add remaining 2 tablespoons olive oil in the skillet and add sliced potatoes. Cook until potatoes are fork tender, about 8 minutes. Stir a few times to avoid potatoes from burning, but stir gently to avoid breaking up the potatoes.
5. Crack eggs in a large bowl, add salt and black pepper, and whisk to combine.
6. Put potatoes and vegetables into the bowl and transfer back to the skillet gently.
7. Bake for 20 minutes or until eggs have set and the tortilla looks slightly golden brown.
8. Let rest before cutting into wedges. Serve warm or at room temperature.

NOTE

If you don't have an ovenproof skillet, simply use a round baking dish.

BROCCOLI EGG MUFFIN CUPS WITH SHARP CHEDDAR

YIELDS 12 cups

PREP 10 minutes   COOK 20 minutes   TOTAL 30 minutes

Ⓝ NUT-FREE

These savory egg muffin cups are wonderful for the lunch box or served at kids' birthday parties. They also make a nutritious breakfast-on-the-go. They are fun to make and easily customizable. If you have silicone muffin tin liners, use them as they will prevent eggs from sticking to the pan.

INGREDIENTS

⅓ cup finely chopped yellow onion
¾ cup finely chopped broccoli florets
12 large pastured eggs
½ teaspoon unrefined salt
¼ teaspoon ground black pepper

Pinch paprika
1 cup organic freshly grated sharp cheddar, Gruyere or dairy-free cheese
Extra-virgin olive oil (optional)

INSTRUCTIONS

1. Preheat oven to 350F.
2. Coat a nonstick muffin pan lightly with olive oil or line with silicone liners. Set aside.
3. Divide onions and broccoli evenly between muffin tins.
4. Whisk eggs, salt, black pepper and paprika together in a medium mixing bowl. Divide egg mixture into the pans, filling each cup about two-thirds full.
5. Top with cheese, if desired.
6. Bake for 20 minutes or until eggs are set.
7. If no silicone liners were used, run a rubber spatula around the edges and lift the egg muffins out gently.
8. Serve warm or at room temperature.

NOTES

- Leftovers can be stored in an airtight container up to four days. Reheat in the oven at 325F until warm or microwave for 30 seconds. They can also be frozen up to one month.
- You can also customize each muffin cups however you would like. Try tomato and basil, spinach and goat cheese or traditional ham and cheese. Just make sure to chop ingredients into bite-sized pieces.
- If you are dairy-free, use dairy-free cheese or simply omit.

EGGS BENEDICT WITH AVOCADO 'HOLLANDAISE'

SERVES 2-4

PREP 15 minutes   COOK 5 minutes   TOTAL 20 minutes

Ⓝ NUT-FREE

Perfect for a weekend morning or a small brunch gathering, this indulgent yet healthy recipe is low in carbohydrates and full of healthy fats and anti-inflammatory properties. The avocado 'hollandaise' is light, creamy, slightly tangy and adds a lovely touch of color to the dish. For a grain-free option, replace the English muffin with a baked portobello mushroom, roasted root vegetables or thick slices of sweet potatoes.

INGREDIENTS

EGGS BENEDICT

4 fresh pastured eggs
White vinegar or apple cider vinegar, for poaching eggs
4 slices whole-grain, sprouted or gluten-free English muffins or slices of bread
8 slices wild smoked salmon
Paprika, to taste
Freshly ground black pepper, to taste
Fresh dill or parsley, minced, for garnish
Drained capers (optional)

AVOCADO 'HOLLANDAISE'

1 large ripe avocado, pitted
2 tablespoons extra-virgin olive oil
2 tablespoons fresh lemon juice
⅓ cup water
½ teaspoon unrefined salt
Pinch cayenne pepper

NOTE

When poaching eggs, it's best to use fresh eggs as the white will be thicker and produce a better shape.

INSTRUCTIONS

1. Make the avocado 'hollandaise.' In a small blender, combine avocado, olive oil, lemon juice, water, salt and cayenne pepper then blend until smooth. Set aside.

2. To poach the eggs, bring a pot of cold water to a boil. Reduce to a simmer – the water should be steamy but not bubbly. Add a splash of vinegar. Break eggs, one at a time, into a small bowl or saucer. Stir the water to create a gentle whirlpool and slide egg into center. Simmer until white is set, about 4 minutes. Remove egg with slotted spoon and drain on kitchen towel. Repeat with remaining eggs. If your pot is large enough, you may poach multiple eggs at once. However, the cooking time will increase slightly.

3. Toast bread until slightly crisp and put on a plate.

4. Top with smoked salmon, poached egg and sprinkle with paprika and black pepper.

5. Drizzle avocado sauce on top, and garnish with capers and dill or parsley if desired. Serve immediately.

SOUTHWEST SCRAMBLED EGGS

SERVES 4

PREP 10 minutes   COOK 15 minutes   TOTAL 25 minutes

Ⓝ NUT-FREE

Lovely for breakfast, lunch or dinner, this flavorful scrambled egg dish is sure to please your family. For a more complete meal, serve it with guacamole, salsa and organic tortillas or tortilla chips. You can even make breakfast burritos by filling tortillas with the egg mixture.

INGREDIENTS

1 tablespoon extra-virgin olive oil

½ cup diced onions

1 clove garlic, minced

½ cup diced green bell peppers

1 cup diced tomatoes (about 1 Roma tomato)

½ teaspoon chili powder

1 teaspoon unrefined salt

Freshly ground black pepper

6 pastured eggs

1 can (15 ounces/425 grams) organic
    black beans, rinsed and drained

1 cup organic shredded cheese, such
    as Mozzarella, Monterey Jack or
    dairy-free cheese (optional)

Sliced green onions, for garnish

Cilantro leaves, for garnish

Hot sauce, for serving (optional)

INSTRUCTIONS

1. Heat olive oil over medium heat in a large skillet.

2. Add onions and garlic, and cook until soft and fragrant, about 3 minutes.

3. Add bell peppers, tomatoes, chili powder, salt and black pepper, and cook until vegetables have softened, about 5 to 6 minutes.

4. Meanwhile, break eggs into a medium mixing bowl and whisk to combine. Set aside.

5. Add black beans to skillet and cook for another 2 minutes.

6. Add eggs and cheese, if using, and scramble the eggs with a spatula constantly until eggs are set.

7. Garnish with green onions and cilantro leaves, and hot sauce, if desired, and serve.

SPINACH QUICHE WITH SWEET POTATO CRUST

SERVES 6-8

PREP 20 minutes   COOK 1 hour, 10 minutes   TOTAL 1 hour, 30 minutes

Ⓝ NUT-FREE

Instead of using dough to make the crust, this recipe uses shredded sweet potatoes. The crust is not as crisp as with a regular dough, but it's much healthier and just as satisfying. The filling is made of eggs, almond milk and spinach. Add organic bacon for a meat option or sliced mushrooms for a vegetarian option. This quiche is very savory. Serve it for brunch with a large mixed salad.

INGREDIENTS

CRUST

1 pound sweet potato (about 1 large), peeled and shredded
1 teaspoon extra-virgin olive oil
½ teaspoon unrefined salt
Pinch red pepper flakes

FILLING

4 slices organic bacon, cut into small pieces, or 1 cup sliced mushrooms
1 cup spinach
8 pastured eggs
¼ cup unsweetened plain almond milk
¼-½ teaspoon unrefined salt
¼ teaspoon freshly ground black pepper

INSTRUCTIONS

1. Preheat oven to 425F.
2. Put shredded sweet potatoes in a colander and squeeze excess water with your hands. Transfer to a large bowl and toss with egg, salt and red pepper flakes.
3. Press shredded potato into a 9-inch tart quiche pan into an even layer along the bottom and up the sides.
4. Bake crust for 30 minutes.
5. Meat option: While the crust is baking, cook bacon in a medium skillet over medium-low heat until crisp. Transfer on paper towel to drain excess fat. Wipe off the skillet with paper towels, leaving just a little bit of fat, and add spinach. Cook until wilted, about a minute.
6. Vegetarian option: In a large skillet over medium-low heat, cook sliced mushrooms in 1 teaspoon of olive oil until soft. Then, add spinach and cook until wilted, about a minute. Set aside.
7. Whisk together the eggs, almond milk, salt and black pepper in a large bowl. If using bacon, use ¼ teaspoon salt; if using vegetables, use ½ teaspoon. Set aside.
8. When crust is cooked, take it out of the oven and decrease temperature to 375F.
9. When oven has reached temperature, add spinach mixture to the quiche, and fold gently into egg mixture.
10. Bake for 30 minutes or until eggs are set. Serve warm or at room temperature.

NOTE

For a richer quiche, use full-fat canned coconut milk instead of almond milk.

SWEET POTATO HASH WITH EGGS

SERVES 2

PREP 10 minutes   COOK 20 minutes   TOTAL 30 minutes

🥜 NUT-FREE

This savory breakfast made with sweet potatoes, mushrooms, spinach and pastured eggs is first cooked in a skillet on the stovetop before being finished in the oven. It's a very nutritious and hearty breakfast that should please both children and adults.

INGREDIENTS

1 tablespoon olive, avocado or coconut oil

1 large sweet potato, peeled and cut into ½-inch cubes (about 2 cups)

½ onion, finely chopped

6 cremini or button mushrooms, stemmed and chopped

½ teaspoon smoked paprika

½ teaspoon ground cumin

¼ teaspoon garlic powder

Unrefined salt, to taste

Freshly ground black pepper, to taste

2 cups spinach or kale

2-3 pastured eggs

Minced parsley, for garnish

Sliced avocado, to serve (optional)

INSTRUCTIONS

1. Preheat oven to 350F.
2. Heat oil in a large ovenproof skillet over medium-low heat.
3. Add sweet potatoes and cook, stirring often, until tender, about 6 to 8 minutes.
4. Add onions and mushrooms, stir in paprika, cumin, garlic powder, salt and black pepper, and cook until onions have softened, about 2 to 3 minutes.
5. Stir in spinach or kale and cook for another minute.
6. Crack eggs on top, sprinkle eggs with salt and black pepper, and put skillet in oven. Cook until eggs are cooked to your liking, about 5 to 8 minutes.
7. Remove from oven, plate, garnish with parsley, and serve with sliced avocado if desired.

NOTE

If you dislike mushrooms, you can replace them with sliced Brussels sprouts or diced bell peppers.

FISH

Fish is a high-protein food that provides a variety of health benefits. It's an excellent source of vitamins A and D as well as minerals iodine and selenium. Fish, especially oily fish, is an excellent source of omega-3 fatty acids, which are essential for brain, heart, eye and skin health as well as to decrease inflammation, which reduces the risk of a variety of chronic diseases. Small fish eaten with the bones – such as sardines, anchovies and canned salmon with bones – are also a rich source of calcium.

Fish is easy to prepare at home and can be enjoyed weekly. Try cooking it the day you purchase it to ensure its freshness as fish is a highly perishable food. Favor fresh or frozen fish over breaded or battered ones. If pregnant, avoid high-mercury and raw fish. The best type of fish to eat will depend upon its mercury and omega-3 fatty acid content as well as its sustainability and provenance. It's usually best to choose domestic over imported fish.

Favor the oily fish, such as herring; mackerel; Pacific sardines; Alaskan, coho, pink or sockeye salmon; rainbow trout; and yellowfin, skipjack or albacore tuna from the United States or Canada. Other great choices are Arctic char; Atlantic pollock; anchovies; black cod; black sea bass; catfish from the U.S.; mahi-mahi from the U.S.; Pacific cod; Pacific halibut; Pacific sole; snapper from Hawaii; striped bass; sole; and tilapia from Canada, U.S., Ecuador and Peru.

Avoid American eel; Atlantic cod; Atlantic halibut; Atlantic salmon; Atlantic sole; Atlantic skate; bluefin, bigeye or imported albacore tuna; Chilean sea bass; grouper; marlin; orange roughy; pangasius; imported catfish; shark; red snapper; sturgeon; and swordfish.

The fish recipes you will find in the next few pages use fish that are high in omega-3s, low in mercury and sustainable.

ALMOND-CRUSTED COD WITH YOGURT TURMERIC SAUCE

SERVES 4

PREP 10 minutes   COOK 15 minutes   TOTAL 25 minutes

This colorful dish is light and easy to make and is perfect for spring or summer. Made with ingredients like fresh cod, almond flour, olive oil, lemon juice, parsley and turmeric, this dish has powerful anti-inflammatory properties. The cod is lovely served with a side of roasted carrots or potatoes, wilted spinach, sautéed asparagus or wild rice.

INGREDIENTS

1½ pounds or 4 (6-ounce) skinless cod fillets
Unrefined salt, to taste
Freshly ground black pepper, to taste
½ cup almond flour
½ teaspoon garlic powder
2 tablespoons olive oil, divided
2 tablespoons grass-fed butter, divided
Minced parsley, for garnish
    Lemon wedges, for serving

YOGURT TURMERIC SAUCE

½ cup plain whole milk yogurt or
    plain almond or coconut yogurt
2 tablespoons fresh lemon juice
¼ teaspoon garlic powder
¼ teaspoon ground turmeric
¼ teaspoon unrefined salt
Freshly ground black pepper

NOTE

If dairy-free, cook fish in olive oil and use almond yogurt for the yogurt sauce. The sauce is also good with red meat, roasted vegetables and salads.

INSTRUCTIONS

1. Make the sauce: Stir yogurt, lemon juice, garlic powder, turmeric, salt and black pepper in a small bowl until well combined. Store in the refrigerator until ready to use.
2. Place almond flour in a large shallow dish and mix in garlic powder.
3. Pat dry fish fillets, season with salt and black pepper, and dredge in the almond flour. Set aside.
4. In a large nonstick skillet, heat 1 tablespoon of olive oil and 1 tablespoon of butter over medium heat.
5. Working in batches if necessary, place fillets upside down without touching each other, and cook until a golden crust forms, about 4 minutes.
6. Turn fillets carefully and cook until done, about 4 or 5 minutes more.
7. Transfer fish to plate lined with paper towel.
8. Repeat steps with remaining fillets, adding more oil and butter as needed.
9. Serve warm garnished with minced parsley with side dishes and yogurt sauce if desired.

BAKED SALMON WITH FRESH HERBS

SERVES 4

PREP 10 minutes   COOK 25 minutes   TOTAL 35 minutes

Ⓝ NUT-FREE

This tasty salmon fillet is coated with a mixture of extra-virgin olive oil, fresh lemon juice, shallots, garlic, fresh parsley and basil. Use a large salmon fillet or buy individual fillets. The fish goes well with a side of steamed broccoli or sautéed green beans or a side of wild rice or rice pilaf.

INGREDIENTS

1 (1½ to 2 pounds) wild salmon fillet, skin on, or 4 (6-ounce) fillets

2 tablespoons extra-virgin olive oil

1 tablespoon fresh lemon juice

1 small shallot, minced

1 clove garlic, minced

1 tablespoon minced fresh Italian parsley

1 tablespoon minced fresh basil

Unrefined salt, to taste

Freshly ground black pepper, to taste

INSTRUCTIONS

1. Preheat oven to 375F.
2. Place salmon, skin side down, into a large baking dish. Season with salt and black pepper. If desired, cut fillet into individual pieces.
3. In a small bowl, mix together olive oil, lemon juice, shallot, garlic, parsley and basil, and lightly season with salt and black pepper.
4. Spread herb mixture on top of fish.
5. Bake for about 20 to 25 minutes or until salmon is cooked through and flakes easily with a fork.
6. Plate and serve.

NOTES

- For variation, try arctic char or rainbow trout. Cooking time, however, may change slightly depending on the thickness of the fish – a thinner fish will cook faster.
- If you don't have shallots, replace with 2 tablespoons of finely diced red onions.

COD LEEK POTATO CASSEROLE

SERVES 4-6

PREP 25 minutes   COOK 25 minutes   TOTAL 50 minutes

This dish is inspired from the traditional Newfoundland dish – cod au gratin – a meal made with cod, béchamel sauce, cheese and breadcrumbs. This version is gluten- and dairy-free and made with leeks and fresh thyme. It's a flavorful and nourishing dish, perfect for fall and winter. Pair it with a side of green beans or steamed broccoli.

INGREDIENTS

1 pound baby yellow potatoes,
    sliced (about 3 cups)
1 tablespoon extra-virgin olive oil
1 leek, white and light green parts
    only, halved and sliced
2 cloves garlic, minced
1½ pounds skinless, boneless cod
Unrefined salt, to taste
Freshly ground black pepper, to taste

SAUCE

2 tablespoons olive oil
2 tablespoons sweet white rice flour or
    gluten-free all-purpose flour
2 cups unsweetened plain almond milk
1 tablespoon fresh thyme leaves
¾ teaspoon unrefined salt
¼ teaspoon ground black pepper
⅛ teaspoon ground nutmeg
2 tablespoons nutritional yeast (optional)

1 cup finely chopped almonds or almond
    breadcrumbs (page 312), to garnish

NOTES

Nutritional yeast adds a slightly 'cheesy' flavor to the sauce. If your family enjoys its taste, try adding it to the sauce.

INSTRUCTIONS

1. Preheat oven to 400F.
2. Place potatoes in a large saucepan and cover with cold water. Bring to a boil, add a pinch of salt and cook until potatoes are tender, about 8 minutes. Drain in a colander. Reserve.
3. While potatoes are cooking, make the sauce. In a small saucepan, heat olive oil over medium-low heat. When hot, add flour and whisk constantly for 1 minute. Whisk in almond milk slowly. Bring mixture to a boil, reduce heat to low and simmer, stirring regularly until sauce has thickened, about 5 minutes. Turn off heat and whisk in thyme, salt, black pepper and nutmeg, and nutritional yeast if using.
4. Heat 1 tablespoon of olive oil in a medium skillet over medium-low heat. Add leeks and garlic, and cook until softened, about 3 to 4 minutes. Remove from heat and set aside.
5. Dice cod and season with salt and black pepper. Place into a large 9x13-inch baking dish. Add potatoes and leeks and cover with the sauce.
6. Top with finely chopped almonds or almond breadcrumbs.
7. Bake uncovered until fish is cooked through and flakes easily, about 20 to 25 minutes.
8. Remove from oven and allow to cool for 5 to 10 minutes before serving.

CRISPY FISH CAKES

YIELDS 10 cakes

PREP 20 minutes   COOK 15 minutes   TOTAL 35 minutes

Crispy fish cakes made with fresh cod, organic potatoes, eggs and almond flour. Serve them with a side of homemade slaw, steamed peas, green beans or wild rice. It's a perfect dish for spring and summer that is light yet satisfying.

INGREDIENTS

½ pound organic potatoes, about 1 medium potato, peeled and chopped

4 tablespoons extra-virgin olive oil, divided

1 pound skinned, boneless white fish fillets (like cod or haddock)

2 pastured eggs, beaten

1 shallot, minced

1 teaspoon Dijon mustard

1 tablespoon minced parsley

1 teaspoon lemon zest

1 teaspoon unrefined salt

¼ teaspoon ground black pepper

½ cup almond flour

Tartar sauce or homemade mayonnaise and lemon wedges, for serving

INSTRUCTIONS

1. Place potatoes in a saucepan and cover with cold water. Add a pinch of salt, bring to a boil and cook until fork tender, about 10 minutes. Drain, return potatoes to pot and mash with a potato masher. Set aside.

2. While potatoes are boiling, heat 1 tablespoon of oil in a large skillet over medium-low heat. Add fish and cook until fish is cooked through and flakes easily, about 10 minutes. Set aside.

3. In a large mixing bowl, whisk the eggs with the shallot, mustard, parsley, lemon zest, salt and black pepper.

4. Add in mashed potatoes, fish, almond flour and 1 tablespoon of olive oil, and stir to combine.

5. Using a ¼ cup measuring scoop, scoop some of the fish mixture and form patties with your hands. Place on a plate.

6. Heat a large nonstick skillet over medium-low heat. Add 1 tablespoon of oil and add as many fish cakes as you can fit in the pan but without them touching together.

7. Cook until golden and crispy, about 4 minutes on one side. Turn the fish cakes and cook for an additional 4 minutes.

8. Put fish cakes on a plate. Wipe out skillet, add another tablespoon of olive oil, and cook remaining patties.

9. Divide fish cakes between plates, and serve with tartar sauce or mayonnaise and lemon wedges if desired, along with side dishes.

FISH STICKS WITH YOGURT TARTAR SAUCE

SERVES 4

PREP 10 minutes   COOK 15 minutes   TOTAL 25 minutes

If you have never made your own fish sticks, it's time to try! You will be surprised by how easy it is to make them and how tasty they are. Fresh fish is cut into sticks, seasoned and dredged with almond flour. The result is fish sticks that are crisp yet healthy, light but satisfying. Serve with yogurt tartar sauce or your favorite healthy fish sauce.

INGREDIENTS

1 pound fresh cod or haddock
    fillets, cut into strips
Unrefined salt, to taste
Freshly ground black pepper, to taste
1 pastured egg
½ cup almond flour
¼ cup arrowroot or tapioca starch

½ teaspoon garlic powder
½ teaspoon onion powder
¼ teaspoon unrefined salt
Pinch cayenne pepper
2-4 tablespoons olive oil, coconut
    oil or clarified butter
Yogurt tartar sauce (page 320), to serve

INSTRUCTIONS

1. Pat dry cod with paper towels, season with salt and black pepper, and cut into sticks, about 1-inch wide and 3 inches long (the width of the fish should be large enough for the length of the sticks).
2. Whisk the egg in a small bowl. Set aside.
3. Combine almond flour, arrowroot, garlic powder, onion powder, salt and cayenne pepper in a medium-sized bowl and stir to combine.
4. Dip cod pieces into the whisked egg and then into the almond flour mixture to coat.
5. Heat butter or oil in a large skillet over medium-low heat. Add fish sticks to skillet, making sure they are not touching. Cook 3 to 4 minutes on each side or until they are cooked through and look crisp and golden brown. Transfer fish to plate lined with paper towel and repeat with remaining cod sticks, adding more butter or oil as needed.
6. Serve with yogurt tartar sauce or your favorite fish sauce.

NOTE

If you don't have arrowroot or tapioca starch, you could use cornstarch but note that the recipe would not be grain-free anymore.

PAN-SEARED SALMON WITH AVOCADO MANGO SALSA

SERVES 4

PREP 15 minutes   COOK 15 minutes   TOTAL 30 minutes

Ⓝ NUT-FREE

Individual salmon fillets are seasoned and seared in a large skillet until golden and crisp. Then, they are topped with a fresh avocado mango salsa. This colorful, refreshing summer dish looks impressive while being very easy to make. Serve the fish with a side of seasonal vegetables and red quinoa, if desired.

INGREDIENTS

1-2 tablespoons avocado oil,
    grapeseed oil or olive oil
4 (6-ounce) wild salmon fillets
Unrefined salt, to taste
Freshly ground black pepper, to taste
Garlic powder, to taste
Smoked paprika, to taste

AVOCADO MANGO SALSA

1 large ripe avocado
¼ cup diced fresh mango
1 teaspoon extra-virgin olive oil
2 teaspoons fresh lime juice
Unrefined salt, to taste
Freshly ground black pepper, to taste

NOTE

Leftover salmon can be stored in an airtight container in the refrigerator for up to three days.

INSTRUCTIONS

1. Take salmon out of the refrigerator about 10 to 15 minutes before starting.
2. Meanwhile, make avocado mango salsa. In a small bowl, combine avocado flesh, diced mango, oil, lime juice, salt and black pepper and stir gently to combine. Set aside.
3. Pat salmon fillets dry with paper towel and season them with salt, black pepper, garlic powder and paprika.
4. Heat a large skillet over medium-high heat. When hot, add oil. When it shimmers, place fillets skin-side down. Cook, without moving the fish, until skin is golden and crisp, and fish is about ¾ cooked through, about 6 to 8 minutes.
5. Flip fillets and reduce heat to medium. Continue cooking until done to your liking, about 2 to 3 minutes more.
6. Rest fillets for 2 minutes before plating.
7. Spoon salsa on top of each fillet and serve with side dishes.

RAINBOW TROUT WITH SPINACH AND SWEET POTATO PURÉE

SERVES 4

PREP 10 minutes   COOK 20 minutes   TOTAL 30 minutes

Ⓝ NUT-FREE

Colorful dish made with rainbow trout, wilted spinach and creamy sweet potato purée. It's simple and easy to make and beautifully delicious.

INGREDIENTS

FISH

4 rainbow trout fillets
Unrefined salt, to taste
Freshly ground black pepper, to taste
1 teaspoon Herbs de Provence, divided
1 tablespoon extra-virgin olive oil

SWEET POTATO PURÉE

2 pounds sweet potatoes, peeled
    and diced (about 3 medium)
2 tablespoons extra-virgin olive oil
1 teaspoon unrefined salt

WILTED SPINACH

2 tablespoons extra-virgin olive oil
8 cups spinach
Unrefined salt, to taste
Ground black pepper, to taste
Red pepper flakes, to taste (optional)

INSTRUCTIONS

1. Place sweet potato in a large pot and fill with cold water. Bring to a boil and cook until potatoes are fork-tender, about 8 minutes. Drain in a colander and transfer potatoes to a food processor. Add olive oil and salt and purée until silky smooth. Set aside.

2. While potatoes are boiling, pat trout fillets with paper towels and season each fillet with salt, pepper and ¼ teaspoon of Herbs de Provence.

3. Heat olive oil in a large skillet over medium heat.

4. Place fish fillets skin side up and sear for 3 minutes. Turn fillets over, reduce heat to medium-low and cook for an additional 4 to 6 minutes or until to your liking.

5. Heat olive oil in a large skillet over medium heat. Add spinach by batches, stirring often until all wilted. Season with salt, pepper and red pepper flakes if using.

6. Divide sweet potatoes between plates, add wilted spinach and place trout fillets on top of spinach.

SEA BASS FILLETS WITH TOMATO CAPER SAUCE

SERVES 4

PREP 10 minutes   COOK 15 minutes   TOTAL 25 minutes

Ⓝ NUT-FREE

Inspired by Mediterranean flavors, this elegant dish uses sea bass, also known as branzino or loup de mer, which is a lean and flaky fish with a sweet and mild flavor. The fish is lovely served with a side of arugula salad, quinoa pilaf or angel hair pasta. If sea bass is not available, look for black cod, snapper, perch or barramundi.

INGREDIENTS

4 skin-on sea bass fillets
Coarse sea salt, to taste
Freshly ground black pepper, to taste
1-2 tablespoons olive oil

TOMATO CAPER SAUCE

1 tablespoon extra-virgin olive oil
¼ cup diced red onion
1 garlic, crushed
2 cups quartered baby tomatoes
¼ teaspoon unrefined salt
⅛ teaspoon freshly ground black pepper
½ teaspoon balsamic vinegar
1 tablespoon capers

NOTE

You can also get a whole sea bass and bake or grill it and spoon the sauce over the fillets.

INSTRUCTIONS

1. Pat sea bass fillets dry and season one side with salt and black pepper. Set aside.
2. Heat oil in a large skillet over medium heat. Place fillets skin-side down and cook until crisp and golden, about 4 minutes. Flip fish carefully and cook until done, about 3 minutes or more, depending on thickness of fish.
3. While fish is cooking, make the sauce. Heat olive oil in a small skillet over medium-low heat. Add red onions and garlic, and cook until soft and fragrant, about 3 minutes. Add tomatoes and season with salt and black pepper. Increase heat and, when it starts to simmer, reduce heat to low and add vinegar and capers. Simmer until tomatoes start to break down, about 3 to 4 minutes. Turn off heat and reserve.
4. Divide fish between plates, spoon sauce over each fillet, and serve.

EASY SOLE MEUNIÈRE

SERVES 4

PREP 10 minutes   COOK 10 minutes   TOTAL 20 minutes

This classic French dish is turned into a healthier version by using almond flour, extra-virgin olive oil and grass-fed butter. Instead of making a rich buttery sauce, a splash of lemon juice is added to the skillet to perfume the fish subtly. The result is a fish that is delicate yet crispy, buttery and slightly lemony. For a more satisfying meal, pair the fish with a bright, colorful French side dish like green beans or steamed new potatoes.

INGREDIENTS

1 pound skinless sole fillets

Unrefined salt, to taste

Freshly ground black pepper, to taste

½ cup almond flour

2 tablespoons extra-virgin olive oil, divided

2 tablespoons grass-fed butter or clarified butter, divided

1 lemon, cut into wedges

Minced parsley, to garnish

INSTRUCTIONS

1. Pat sole fillets dry with paper towels and season with salt and pepper.
2. Dredge fillets on both sides with almond flour. Shake off excess. Set aside in a plate.
3. Heat 1 tablespoon of olive oil and 1 tablespoon of butter in a large nonstick skillet over medium heat. When butter is melted, and foam subsides, add fish and cook until golden brown on bottom, about 2 to 3 minutes. Turn fish over carefully, take a wedge of lemon and add a splash of lemon juice to the skillet, and cook fish until opaque in center and golden on bottom, about 2 minutes more. Transfer fish to plates.
4. Wipe skillet with paper towels. Add remaining tablespoon of oil and butter and repeat steps to cook remaining fillets.
5. Divide fish between plates, garnish with minced parsley and freshly ground black pepper if desired, and serve with remaining lemon wedges.

NOTE

If you can't tolerate dairy, use clarified butter (also known as ghee) instead. It's lactose- and casein-free. For a dairy-free option, cook in olive oil only.

SWEET POTATO TUNA PATTIES

YIELDS 16 small patties or 8 large patties

PREP 15 minutes   COOK 30 minutes   TOTAL 45 minutes

Ⓝ NUT-FREE

Tuna is a great source of complete protein, vitamin B12, selenium and omega-3 fatty acids. Made with chunk light tuna, mashed sweet potatoes, garlic, and parsley, these baked patties are very flavorful and satisfying. Serve the patties with a side of greens, crudités or avocado and sauce, if desired. For variation, try making tuna burgers with the patties.

INGREDIENTS

1 medium sweet potato, about
    ¾ pound, peeled and diced
2 cans (5 ounces/142 grams) water-packed wild
    chunk light tuna (Skipjack or Tongol), drained
1 pastured egg or 2 egg yolks
2 tablespoons extra-virgin olive oil
6 scallions, thinly sliced
1 clove garlic, minced
2 tablespoons minced parsley
½ teaspoon unrefined salt
¼ teaspoon red pepper flakes

Yogurt tartar sauce (page 320) or
    cashew aioli (page 312), to serve

INSTRUCTIONS

1. Preheat oven to 350F.
2. Line a large baking sheet with parchment paper. Set aside.
3. Steam or boil sweet potatoes until fork tender, about 10 minutes. Drain, return to pot, and mash using a potato masher. Set aside.
4. In a large bowl, add tuna and flake it with your hands. Add egg or egg yolks, olive oil, scallions, garlic, parsley, salt, and red pepper flakes. Stir to combine and add in mashed sweet potato. Stir well.
5. Scoop out ¼ cup of the mixture on the baking sheet (or 2 tablespoons for smaller servings), and lightly press with your hands to form patties.
6. Bake for 30 minutes or until the edges look crisp.
7. Serve warm.

NOTE

If there is an egg allergy in your family, you can omit.
It will slightly alter the taste and texture, but the patties will still work beautifully.

MEAT AND POULTRY

Animal products are body-building and warming foods. They provide important nutrients, such as vitamins A, B12 and D, and minerals like iron, zinc and selenium. They are a complete source of proteins and provide healthy fats that, contrary to many people's belief, nourish the body – including the brain. Meat can be a very healthy food, depending on its quality and the way it's cooked.

The quality of the meat is very important. Favor meat that is organic, grass-fed and local. If your butcher, grocery store or health food store doesn't carry it, ask for it. You can always visit your area farmers' market or contact a local farm. When you purchase directly from the farm, you also have the advantage of having access to organ meats and bones. Organ meats are very nutritious and healing and bones make excellent stocks.

With poultry, do not neglect to eat the skin or dark meat. The skin provides both unsaturated and saturated fats while the dark meat contains more minerals than white meat. Remember that fats don't make us fat and nature provided us everything we need to nourish our body. Whenever possible, purchase and cook poultry whole so that you can benefit from everything that the animal has to offer.

The way you cook meat matters. It's important to favor cooking methods that minimize nutrient loss and antioxidants and produce the lowest amount of harmful chemicals. High-heat cooking methods, such as deep frying, broiling, and grilling, should be avoided. They can create chemicals that may cause changes in DNA and increase the risk of several diseases and cancer. Those compounds include heterocyclic amines (HCAs), polycyclic hydrocarbons (PAHs), and advanced glycation end-products (AGEs).

Low-heat cooking methods like simmering, poaching and stewing as well as slow cooking, pressure cooking and sous vide are favorable. These are the healthiest cooking methods. Baking and roasting are also healthy choices. Marinating the meat is a beneficial way to prepare meat as it tenderizes the meat, and it also predigests it. The acids in the marinade, such as lemon juice or vinegar, also help decrease AGEs formation.

CHICKEN SAUSAGE SKILLET WITH CAULIFLOWER RICE

SERVES 4

PREP 10 minutes   COOK 25 minutes   TOTAL 35 minutes

Ⓝ NUT-FREE

I wanted to create a healthy 'fried rice' recipe, but minus the rice and soy, so I came up with this fusion meal combining both Asian and French cuisine. It's low in carbohydrates, high in proteins and allergen-free. It's different yet very flavorful and satisfying. Give it a try — you won't be disappointed.

INGREDIENTS

3 tablespoons extra-virgin olive oil, divided

1 package (12 ounces/340 grams)
   organic chicken sausages,
   casings removed and sliced

1 small onion, diced

2 cloves garlic, minced

¾ cup diced celery, about 2 stalks

¾ cup diced carrots, about 2 medium carrots

¾ cup frozen peas

¼ teaspoon dried thyme

¼ teaspoon smoked paprika

1 medium head cauliflower, cut into florets

1 ½ teaspoon unrefined salt

Freshly ground black pepper

2 tablespoons minced fresh parsley,
   plus more for garnish

Lemon wedges, to serve

INSTRUCTIONS

1. In a large skillet over medium heat, brown sausages in 1 tablespoon of olive oil until cooked through, about 6 to 8 minutes. Set aside.

2. Meanwhile, in a large pot, add 1 tablespoon of olive oil and sauté onions and garlic until soft and fragrant, about 3 minutes.

3. Add carrots, celery, and peas as well as thyme and paprika, and cook until vegetables are tender, about 6 minutes.

4. While the vegetables are cooking, put cauliflower florets into a food processor. Pulse a few times for a few seconds each time, scraping sides as needed, until you get the consistency of rice.

5. Transfer cauliflower rice to the pot, season with salt and black pepper, and add another tablespoon of olive oil. Stir to combine and cook until cauliflower rice is warm and soft, about 6 minutes.

6. Add sausages and parsley to pot, stir to combine, turn off heat, and let cook for another 2 minutes before serving.

7. Garnish with parsley and serve with lemon wedges.

CHICKEN TENDERS WITH HONEY MUSTARD DIPPING SAUCE

SERVES 2-4

PREP 10 minutes   COOK 15 minutes   TOTAL 25 minutes

ⓘ NUT-FREE OPTION

These healthy chicken tenders are coated with a grain-free almond flour crust, pan-fried until crisp and served with a sweet honey mustard sauce. They are a fun, healthy and delicious way to serve chicken to your children. Complete the meal with a healthy starch and vegetable, such as sweet potato fries or mashed cauliflower 'potatoes,' and steamed peas or broccoli.

INGREDIENTS

1 cup almond flour or gluten-free all-purpose flour

1 teaspoon paprika

1 teaspoon onion powder

¾ teaspoon unrefined salt

½ teaspoon garlic powder

½ teaspoon ground black pepper

¼ teaspoon cayenne powder

2 pastured eggs

1 pound organic boneless skinless chicken breasts or chicken tenderloins

2-3 tablespoons olive oil, coconut oil, or grass-fed butter

DIPPING SAUCE

¼ cup Dijon mustard

¼ cup raw or local honey

INSTRUCTIONS

1. Combine flour, paprika, onion powder, salt, garlic powder, black pepper and cayenne pepper in a shallow bowl. Set aside.
2. In another shallow bowl, beat eggs.
3. Pat dry chicken and cut into strips.
4. Dip the chicken strips one by one lightly into the beaten eggs, and then into the flour mixture. Shake off excess and place on a plate.
5. Heat oil or butter in a large skillet over medium-low heat. Add chicken strips and cook until they begin to brown and the chicken is cooked halfway through, about 4 to 5 minutes. Then, flip chicken and cook for a few more minutes until cooked through.
6. Wipe off skillet and repeat steps with remaining chicken, adding more oil or butter as needed.
7. Make the dipping sauce by whisking together the mustard and honey in a small bowl.
8. Serve chicken strips with dipping sauce and side dishes.

GLAZED MAPLE SOY CHICKEN THIGHS

SERVES 4

PREP 15 minutes   COOK 45 minutes   TOTAL 1 hour

Ⓝ NUT-FREE

Chicken thighs are a cut of dark meat that is very tender and flavorful. They are also richer in minerals than chicken breasts and more economical too. I used boneless, skinless chicken thighs in the recipe, but skin-on chicken thighs work as well. Serve this Asian-inspired dish with basmati rice or riced cauliflower and sautéed bok choy, snow peas or broccoli.

INGREDIENTS

1½ pounds organic boneless, skinless chicken thighs (about 8 chicken thighs), fat trimmed

¼ cup gluten-free tamari

¼ cup pure maple syrup

2 tablespoons sesame oil

2 tablespoons lime juice

2 cloves garlic, minced

1 teaspoon freshly grated ginger

⅛ teaspoon red pepper flakes

1 tablespoon arrowroot starch

1 tablespoon water

NOTE

Arrowroot is a healthier thickener but gives a slimier texture, which may not be appealing for some. You can also try tapioca starch, kuzu root or organic cornstarch, using an equal amount when substituting.

INSTRUCTIONS

1. Combine tamari, maple syrup, sesame oil, lime juice, garlic, ginger and red pepper flakes in a large container and add chicken thighs. Cover, refrigerate and marinate for at least 1 hour or overnight.

2. Preheat oven to 400F and line a large baking sheet with aluminum foil and parchment paper.

3. Remove chicken thighs from marinade, shake off excess and place on baking sheet. Reserve marinade.

4. Bake chicken until crisp, about 45 minutes.

5. While chicken is baking, put marinade in a small saucepan. Bring the marinade to a boil, reduce heat to medium to simmer and cook for 10 minutes. Turn off heat. Mix starch with water in a small bowl and add it to the sauce. Whisk to combine and set aside.

6. Remove chicken from oven and brush chicken generously with sauce.

7. Serve 2 to 3 chicken thighs per person along with side dishes.

GREEK-STYLE LAMB TENDERLOIN KEBABS

SERVES 4

PREP 20 minutes   COOK 15 minutes   TOTAL 35 minutes

Ⓝ NUT-FREE

Lamb tenderloin is a perfect cut for kebabs – it's very tender. The meat is first marinated in a Greek-style marinade before being thread onto skewers. The kebabs are baked but are perfect for the grill too. If adding vegetables to the skewers, cut them the same size as the meat. You can also make extra vegetable skewers. Serve with warm pita bread, tzatziki sauce and salad.

INGREDIENTS

LAMB & MARINADE
¼ cup extra-virgin olive oil
2 tablespoons fresh lemon juice
2 cloves garlic, crushed
1 teaspoon dried oregano
1 teaspoon unrefined salt
½ teaspoon ground black pepper
1-1½ pounds lamb tenderloin, fat trimmed

OPTIONAL VEGETABLES
1 bell pepper, cut into squares
1 small red onion, cut into squares
1 small zucchini, thickly sliced
6-8 cherry tomatoes
4 button or cremini mushrooms, quartered
1 tablespoon olive oil
Unrefined salt, to taste
Ground black pepper, to taste

OPTIONAL SIDES
Pita bread
Tzatziki sauce, preferably homemade
Salad, such as Greek salad, couscous or tabbouleh

1. Combine olive oil, lemon juice, garlic, oregano, salt and black pepper in a closed container or a resealable plastic bag.
2. Cut meat into 1-inch cubes. Add meat to the container or plastic bag with the marinade. Toss to coat, cover or seal and marinate in the refrigerator for 1 to 4 hours.
3. If using bamboo skewers, soak them in water for 30 minutes before cooking.
4. Preheat oven to 400F.
5. Remove lamb from refrigerator to bring meat to room temperature.
6. If using vegetables, place vegetables in a medium mixing bowl, toss with oil and season with salt and black pepper. Set aside.
7. Remove the cubes of lamb out of the marinade and thread onto metal or soaked bamboo skewers. If adding vegetables to skewers, alternate with vegetables. You can also make skewers using vegetables only.
8. Place skewers on a large baking sheet and bake in the oven for 12 minutes or until cooked to your liking. If making vegetable skewers only, start them 10 to 15 minutes ahead, so vegetables are more tender.
9. Let meat rest for 2 to 3 minutes before serving.
10. Serve skewers with warm pita bread, homemade tzatziki or plain yogurt and a Greek salad, couscous or tabbouleh if desired.

NOTE

Frozen lamb tenderloin works beautifully in the recipe. Defrost it in the refrigerator. You can also use leg of lamb or lamb shoulder in the recipe.

LEMON THYME CHICKEN

SERVES 2-4

PREP 20 minutes   COOK 40 minutes   TOTAL 1 hour

(⬤) NUT-FREE

This colorful, light and nutritious chicken dish is perfect for spring and summer. Serve it with a side of red quinoa and sautéed asparagus if desired. Use two to four chicken breasts, depending on how big they are. If you have leftover chicken, slice it and add it to sandwiches or salads.

INGREDIENTS

2 to 4 organic boneless chicken breasts
Unrefined salt, to taste
Freshly ground black pepper, to taste
2 tablespoons olive oil
1 shallot, finely diced
4 cloves garlic, minced

½ teaspoon dried thyme
Pinch red pepper flakes
Zest of 1 small lemon, about 1 tablespoon
½ cup chicken broth
Lemon slices, for garnish (optional)
Thyme sprigs, for garnish (optional)

INSTRUCTIONS

1. Preheat oven to 400F.
2. Season chicken breasts with salt and black pepper and place on a plate.
3. Heat a large skillet over medium-high heat and add olive oil.
4. Sear chicken breasts for about 3 minutes or until chicken releases from pan easily and has a nice golden color. Place chicken breasts in a baking dish.
5. Reduce heat to low, add shallots, garlic, thyme and red pepper flakes to the skillet and cook, until fragrant, about 2 minutes.
6. Turn off heat and add lemon zest and broth.
7. Stir and pour sauce over chicken breasts.
8. Add a slice of lemon and a sprig of fresh thyme on chicken breasts if desired.
9. Cover with aluminum foil for 20 minutes, then remove foil and bake for an additional 20 minutes or until chicken is cooked through.
10. Remove chicken from oven and let rest for 5 minutes before serving or slicing.
11. Spoon cooking liquid over chicken breasts, add freshly ground black pepper to taste and serve with side dishes.

NOTE

Cooking time will vary depending on the thickness of the chicken breasts.

MOM'S SPAGHETTI SAUCE

SERVES 10

PREP 30 minutes   COOK 3 hours   TOTAL 3 hours, 30 minutes

Ⓝ NUT-FREE

When I was growing up, one of the best food memories I have is the smell and taste of my mom's spaghetti sauce – chunky, hearty and so comforting. I tried to make something similar as I don't have her recipe, and I'm extremely pleased with the result. My family loves it, and I'm sure yours will too. This is the only meat sauce you'll ever need!

INGREDIENTS

2 tablespoons extra-virgin olive oil
1 medium onion, finely chopped
4 cloves garlic, minced
1 cup diced carrots
1 cup diced celery
1 tablespoon dried basil
1 teaspoon dried oregano
1 teaspoon dried marjoram
¼ teaspoon crushed red pepper flakes
2 bay leaves
1½ teaspoon unrefined salt
¼ teaspoon ground black pepper
1½ to 2 pounds grass-fed ground beef
2 cans (12 ounces/340 grams each) tomato paste

1 (28 ounces/794 grams) can crushed tomatoes, preferably San Marzano
2 cans (15 ounces/425 grams each) tomato sauce
1 tablespoon coconut sugar
½ cup water
¼ cup red wine, such as cabernet sauvignon, merlot or pinot noir (optional)

Favorite Italian, gluten-free pasta or zucchini noodles, to serve
Freshly grated parmesan cheese, to garnish (optional)

INSTRUCTIONS

1. In a large, heavy stockpot, add olive oil over medium-low heat.
2. Add onions and garlic, and cook until softened, about 3 minutes.
3. Stir in carrots, celery, basil, oregano, marjoram, red pepper flakes and bay leaves. Cook, stirring occasionally, until vegetables have softened, about 8 minutes.
4. Add meat, breaking it up as you stir with a wooden spatula, and cook until meat is mostly cooked but not thoroughly, about 8 minutes.
5. Stir in tomato paste and let it brown slightly.
6. Add crushed tomatoes, tomato sauce, coconut sugar, water and red wine if using. Stir well and bring to a boil.
7. Reduce heat to low, partially cover and simmer for 2 to 3 hours, stirring frequently to avoid the sauce from burning.
8. Cook pasta according to package directions.
9. Remove bay leaves, spoon sauce over pasta and garnish with freshly grated parmesan cheese if desired.

SHEET PAN HONEY DIJON CHICKEN WITH VEGETABLES

SERVES 4

PREP 15 minutes   COOK 40 minutes   TOTAL 55 minutes

Ⓝ NUT-FREE

Sheet pan dinners are ideal for busy weeknight meals. They are easy to make while providing satisfying results. This dish is a combination of chicken – breasts or thighs – cooked with a flavorful mild honey Dijon sauce along with baby potatoes, carrots, Brussels sprouts and red onions. It is a complete meal as is.

INGREDIENTS

1½ pounds chicken breasts or
   boneless chicken thighs
Unrefined salt, to taste
Freshly ground black pepper, to taste

SAUCE

¼ cup organic, local honey
2 tablespoons whole grain mustard
1 tablespoon Dijon mustard
1 tablespoon extra-virgin olive oil
2 cloves garlic, minced
1 teaspoon fresh thyme leaves
Pinch red pepper flakes

VEGETABLES

1 pound red or assorted baby potatoes, halved
½ pound Brussels sprouts, halved
   lengthwise (about 2 cups)
2 carrots, sliced
1 small red onion, peeled and cut into quarters
2 tablespoons extra-virgin olive oil
Unrefined salt, to taste
Freshly ground black pepper, to taste

INSTRUCTIONS

1. Preheat oven to 400F.
2. Place chicken on a large nonstick baking sheet and season with salt and black pepper.
3. Whisk together honey, mustard, olive oil, garlic, thyme and red pepper flakes in a small bowl until well combined. Set aside.
4. Combine potatoes, Brussels sprouts, carrots, and onions in a large mixing bowl. Toss in olive oil and season with salt and black pepper to taste.
5. Arrange vegetables around the chicken in a single layer. If there is not enough space on your baking sheet, place chicken breasts over vegetables.
6. Brush sauce generously over chicken.
7. Bake for 40 minutes or until chicken is cooked through and vegetables look tender and caramelized. If you want the chicken to be crispier on top, broil for a few minutes.
8. Divide chicken, potatoes, and vegetables between plates, garnish with fresh thyme if desired, and serve.

SLOW COOKER CHICKEN TIKKA MASALA

SERVES 2-4

PREP 10 minutes   COOK 4 or 6 hours   TOTAL 4 hours, 10 minutes or 6 hours, 10 minutes

Ⓝ NUT-FREE

A warming and comforting slow cooker recipe featuring Indian flavors, this chicken tikka masala is very flavorful while being dairy-free and easy to make. Enjoy with rice or naan bread for a complete meal.

INGREDIENTS

1 ½ pound organic chicken breasts or thighs, chopped
1 medium onion, diced
2 cloves garlic, minced
1 tablespoon freshly grated ginger
¼ cup tomato paste
1 tablespoon ground cumin
½ teaspoon paprika
½ teaspoon curry powder
¼ teaspoon ground coriander

¼ teaspoon ground cinnamon
Pinch cayenne pepper
1 teaspoon unrefined salt
¼ teaspoon ground black pepper
1 can (13.5 ounces/400 milliliters) full-fat coconut milk
1 tablespoon fresh lemon juice
¼ cup chopped cilantro
Cooked jasmine or basmati rice, cauliflower rice or naan bread, to serve

INSTRUCTIONS

1. Place chicken, onions, garlic and ginger in your slow cooker.
2. In a small bowl, whisk together the tomato paste, cumin, paprika, curry powder, coriander, cinnamon, cayenne, salt, black pepper and coconut milk.
3. Add sauce to slow cooker, stir, and cook on low for 6 hours or on high for 4 hours.
4. When done cooking, turn off heat, and stir in lemon juice and cilantro.
5. Serve over rice or with naan bread.

UNSTUFFED CABBAGE ROLLS

SERVES 4

PREP 10 minutes   COOK 40 minutes   TOTAL 50 minutes

🥜 NUT-FREE

Easier and quicker to make than traditional cabbage rolls, this recipe is a combination of ground beef, tomatoes, cabbage and aromatics that are all cooked together in one large pot. Rice can be added to the dish, but it's incredibly flavorful and satisfying without it. It's a very hearty meal that is ideal to make during the cooler months of the year.

INGREDIENTS

1 tablespoon olive oil

1 small yellow onion, finely chopped

2 cloves garlic, minced

⅛ teaspoon ground nutmeg

Pinch red pepper flakes

1 pound grass-fed ground beef

1 can (14.5 ounces/411 grams) diced tomatoes

1 can (8 ounces/227 grams) tomato sauce

½ small green cabbage head, outer leaves removed and chopped (about 4 cups)

1 teaspoon unrefined salt

¼ teaspoon ground black pepper

½ cup dry basmati rice or brown rice (optional)

Minced parsley, to garnish (optional)

INSTRUCTIONS

1. Heat oil over medium-low heat in a large pot or Dutch oven.

2. Add onions and garlic, and cook until soft and fragrant, about 3 minutes.

3. Add nutmeg and red pepper flakes, stir and let cook another minute.

4. Add meat and cook until mostly cooked through, breaking down the meat as you stir with a wooden spatula.

5. Add tomatoes and tomato sauce, and stir in cabbage, salt and black pepper.

6. Bring to a boil, reduce heat to low, cover, and simmer until cabbage is tender, about 40 minutes. Divide between plates, garnish with parsley if desired and serve.

7. If using rice, prepare it while cabbage is cooking. When cooked, stir rice into the pot and serve, or divide rice between plates and serve meat on top. Garnish with parsley if desired.

SWEET POTATO SHEPHERD'S PIE

SERVES 6-8

PREP 15 minutes   COOK 1 hour   TOTAL 1 hour, 15 minutes

Ⓝ NUT-FREE

One of America's favorites, shepherd's pie is true comfort food for many. This version is slightly different but just as delicious, if not better. It doesn't contain corn, milk or white potatoes. Instead, it's made with a mixture of onions, carrots, peas, meat and seasonings and a velvety sweet potato layer. It's moist, creamy, nutritious and satisfying.

INGREDIENTS

FILLING

1 tablespoon grass-fed butter or extra-virgin olive oil
1 medium onion, diced
3 cloves garlic, minced
1 cup diced carrots
1 cup frozen peas
½ teaspoon chili powder
2 teaspoons fresh thyme leaves
1 teaspoon unrefined salt

3 tablespoons tomato paste
1½ pounds grass-fed ground beef, lamb, or veal

SWEET POTATO LAYER

2 pounds sweet potatoes, peeled and diced (about 3 medium)
2 tablespoons grass-fed butter or extra-virgin olive oil
1 teaspoon unrefined salt
Smoked paprika, to garnish

INSTRUCTIONS

1. Preheat oven to 400F.
2. In a large pot, heat butter or oil over medium-low heat. Add onions and garlic and cook until translucent, about 5 minutes. Add carrots, peas, chili powder, thyme and salt, and cook until vegetables have softened, about 8 more minutes.
3. Stir in tomato paste and cook for a minute.
4. Add meat and cook, breaking up the meat as you stir, until meat is cooked through, about 8 minutes.
5. Meanwhile, boil sweet potatoes in a pot of salted water until fork-tender, about 12 minutes. Drain in a colander.
6. Transfer potatoes to a food processor. Add butter or oil and salt and purée until silky smooth. Set aside.
7. Add the meat and vegetable mixture in a 9x13-inch baking dish and press firmly with your hands or a spatula. Then, spread the mashed sweet potatoes gently all over the meat. Sprinkle with smoked paprika.
8. Bake for 20 to 25 minutes or until potatoes start to brown.
9. Let cool for 10 minutes before cutting and serving.

NOTE

Leftovers can be kept in the refrigerator up to four days or frozen for four to six months.

THAI RED CURRY GROUND BEEF

SERVES 4

PREP 10 minutes | COOK 15 minutes | TOTAL 25 minutes

Ⓝ NUT-FREE

A colorful and flavorful ground beef dish made with Thai red curry paste, vegetables, basil and lime juice. Easy and quick to make, this meal is perfect as a busy weeknight dinner. Serve it over jasmine rice for a more satisfying meal, or cauliflower rice for a grain-free and low-carbohydrate meal.

INGREDIENTS

1 tablespoon coconut oil

1 small onion, diced

2 large cloves garlic, minced

1 pound grass-fed ground beef

2 tablespoons Thai red curry paste

1 cup matchstick carrots

½ red or yellow bell pepper, thinly sliced

½ cup snow peas, trimmed and
    cut in half on the bias

1 teaspoon unrefined salt

¼ cup lightly packed minced Thai
    basil, plus more to garnish

½ lime, juiced

2 scallions, sliced, for garnish

Cooked jasmine rice or cauliflower rice, to serve

INSTRUCTIONS

1. In a large skillet or pot, heat oil over medium heat.
2. Add onions and garlic, and sauté until soft and fragrant, about 2 minutes.
3. Stir in beef and red curry paste and cook, breaking up meat as you stir, until beef is mostly cooked through but still pink inside, about 8 minutes.
4. Add carrots, bell peppers, snow peas and salt, stir, cover with a lid and cook until vegetables are tender, and meat is cooked through, about 5-6 minutes.
5. Turn off heat and stir in basil and lime juice.
6. Serve over jasmine or cauliflower rice and garnish with sliced scallions and fresh basil, if desired.

NOTE

Try adding a little lime zest and Himalayan salt to the rice or cauliflower rice when cooking. It perfumes the rice delicately, and the result is delicious.
If Thai basil isn't available, use regular basil.

TURKEY MEATBALLS

YIELDS 14-16 meatballs

PREP 10 minutes   COOK 25 minutes   TOTAL 35 minutes

Ⓝ NUT-FREE

These turkey meatballs are free from gluten, grain, milk, soy, and corn. They are started on the stovetop and finished in the oven. If you like, enjoy them with your favorite tomato sauce and pasta. Otherwise, they are delicious served on a bed of mashed potatoes or mashed cauliflower or served with seasonal vegetables.

INGREDIENTS

1 pastured egg

½ small onion, finely chopped

3 cloves garlic, minced

2 tablespoons tomato paste

1/3 cup minced fresh Italian parsley

1 teaspoon dried oregano

1 teaspoon unrefined salt

¼ teaspoon ground black pepper

⅛ teaspoon red pepper flakes

1 pound grass-fed ground dark turkey meat

2 to 4 tablespoons olive oil, coconut
    oil, or grass-fed butter

2 tablespoons coconut flour (optional)

TOMATO SAUCE (PAGE 319), TO SERVE (OPTIONAL)

Favorite healthy pasta, spaghetti
    squash or vegetable 'noodles' or
    mashed potatoes, to serve

INSTRUCTIONS

1. Preheat oven to 400F.
2. In a large bowl, whisk the egg. Stir in onions, garlic, tomato paste, parsley, oregano, salt, black pepper, red pepper flakes and coconut flour if using.
3. Add meat and mix until well combined.
4. In a large skillet, heat oil over medium-high heat. Using a medium ice cream scoop, form meatballs and cook them for about 30 seconds on both sides. You want to get a nice golden color on both sides, but you don't want to cook them all the way through.
5. Transfer meatballs to a baking sheet. Bake for 20 minutes.
6. Serve with your favorite healthy pasta or noodles and with or without sauce.

NOTE

Coconut flour is used as a binder, but the meatballs still work beautifully without it.

VEGETARIAN

In the next few pages, you will find 15 healthy vegetarian recipes featuring different ingredients and flavor profiles. They are very nutritious and flavorful, and most of them are easy to make. Some recipes are common while some are more unusual. Give them a try – you might be very surprised by how tasty and satisfying they are. They are also a terrific way to experiment and introduce new taste and flavors to your family.

My goal is not to transform you into a vegetarian but to have you consume more food from the plant kingdom. I am not referring to processed, refined vegetarian food but real, wholesome food. These foods include fresh fruits, starchy and nonstarchy vegetables, sea vegetables, whole grains, pseudo-grains, legumes and nuts and seeds – food in their natural form. Those types of food are full of vitamins, minerals, fibers, healthy fats, enzymes, antioxidants and phytochemicals that promote health and reduce the risk of many chronic illnesses. Of course, not only eating more from plants is beneficial for your health, but also for animal welfare and the environment.

Changing and balancing our diet is not always easy and often requires developing new tastes, but it can be done and can truly have a positive impact on our lives.

BAKED FALAFELS

YIELDS 15 falafels

PREP 15 minutes   COOK 40 minutes   TOTAL 55 minutes

Ⓝ NUT-FREE

These falafels are baked instead of fried and are ideal served with hummus, tahini sauce, pita bread and an Israeli-type salad if desired. You can also make sandwiches with the pita bread if you prefer. This healthy vegetarian recipe should please the whole family!

INGREDIENTS

1 can (15 ounces/425 grams) chickpeas, rinsed and drained
½ red onion, chopped
2 cloves garlic, chopped
¼ cup fresh parsley
¼ cup fresh cilantro
¼ cup chickpea flour
1 tablespoon extra-virgin olive oil, plus more for brushing
1 tablespoon fresh lemon juice
1 teaspoon ground cumin
1 teaspoon ground coriander
1 teaspoon unrefined salt
Pinch cayenne pepper

OPTIONAL SIDES

Hummus, prepared or homemade (page 237)
Tahini sauce (page 321)
Whole wheat pita bread
Tomato cucumber salad

INSTRUCTIONS

1. Preheat oven to 375F, and line a large baking sheet with parchment paper. Set aside.
2. Add chickpeas, red onion, garlic, parsley, cilantro, chickpea flour, olive oil, lemon juice, cumin, coriander, salt and cayenne pepper in a food processor and pulse a few times until thoroughly combined, scraping down sides as needed with a spatula. Don't overprocess as you want the mixture to hold together but not be completely smooth.
3. Use 2 tablespoons of the falafel mixture and with your hands, form balls and place them on the baking sheet. You can also use a falafel making scoop or a meat baller if you have one.
4. Brush the falafels with olive oil slightly.
5. Bake for 30 to 40 minutes, flipping them halfway through.
6. Allow to cool and serve with side dishes.

NOTES

If making homemade hummus, tahini sauce and/or salad, make while falafels are baking. You can also make them ahead of time.

BUDDHA BOWL WITH MAPLE-TAHINI SAUCE

SERVES 2-4

PREP 10 minutes   COOK 45 minutes   TOTAL 55 minutes

(🥜) NUT-FREE

Buddha bowls are one of my favorite meals. They are so versatile. You can put anything you like in them. This recipe is more kid-friendly, using black beans, brown rice, sweet potatoes and broccoli. The sauce is creamy and slightly sweet, made with maple syrup and tahini. This bowl of goodness is full of colors, flavors and texture.

INGREDIENTS

2 cups water
1 cup dry basmati brown rice or quinoa, rinsed
¼ teaspoon unrefined salt, divided
1 large sweet potato, peeled and diced
1 tablespoon extra-virgin olive oil
1 can (15 ounces/425 grams) black beans, rinsed and drained
½ teaspoon ground cumin
¼ teaspoon garlic powder
¼ teaspoon paprika
½ head broccoli, cut into florets

MAPLE-TAHINI SAUCE
¼ cup tahini
½ lemon, juiced
¼ cup filtered water
1 tablespoon pure maple syrup or local honey
½ teaspoon unrefined salt
¼ teaspoon garlic powder
¼ teaspoon ground cumin
Pinch red pepper flakes

TOPPINGS
1 avocado, sliced
Sesame seeds
Cilantro leaves

INSTRUCTIONS

1. Preheat oven to 400F and line a baking sheet with parchment paper. Set aside.
2. In a small saucepan, bring water to a boil. Add rice or quinoa and a pinch of salt. When it starts boiling again, bring to a simmer, cover, and let cook until water is absorbed, about 40 minutes for brown rice or 20 minutes for quinoa.
3. Toss sweet potatoes with olive oil and a pinch of salt in a medium mixing bowl, then spread potatoes in one single layer on the baking sheet. Roast in oven for about 35 to 40 minutes. Reserve.
4. Meanwhile, in a large skillet over medium-low heat, add olive oil. Stir in beans, cumin, garlic, paprika and a pinch of salt. Cook, stirring frequently until beans are warmed through, about 8 to 10 minutes.
5. Bring a small pot of water to a boil. Add a pinch of salt and stir in broccoli. Boil until tender but not mushy, about 3 minutes. Drain in a colander and reserve.
6. Make the sauce: In a small blender, put the tahini, lemon juice, water, maple syrup, salt, garlic powder, cumin and red pepper flakes. Blend until smooth. Reserve.
7. Assemble the bowls: Put grains at the bottom or on one side of the bowl, then add sweet potatoes, beans and broccoli. Top with avocado, drizzle with sauce and garnish with sesame seeds and cilantro leaves. Alternatively, you can mix up everything in the bowl with the sauce.

NOTES

- To save time, you can roast the broccoli with the sweet potatoes. Add them when potatoes are halfway done cooking as broccoli roast in about 20 minutes.
- For stronger flavors, substitute garlic powder for a small clove of garlic.
  The sauce is also very flavorsome with a little freshly grated ginger added to it.

ZUCCHINI FRITTERS

PREP 15 minutes   COOK 10 minutes   TOTAL 25 minutes

Ⓝ NUT-FREE

Perfect for summer, these fritters are light and nutritious and a fun and pleasant way to eat zucchini. They are tender from the inside and crisp from the outside. The tip to get the fritters as crispy as possible is to extract as much water out as possible from the zucchini. Enjoy them with cashew sour cream or aioli, along with side dishes.

INGREDIENTS

1½ pound zucchini (about 2 medium), shredded
1 pastured egg, beaten
½ cup chickpea flour, oat flour or quinoa flour
2 green onions, thinly sliced
1 clove garlic, minced
1 tablespoon minced parsley
1 teaspoon lemon zest
¾ teaspoon unrefined salt
Freshly ground black pepper
2-4 tablespoons avocado oil, olive oil
    or coconut oil, for pan frying

Cashew sour cream (page 313) or
    cashew aioli (page 312), to serve

NOTE

You can also serve the patties with hummus, baba ganoush or tahini sauce.

INSTRUCTIONS

1. Put shredded zucchini in a colander with a pinch of salt and let sit for 10 minutes. Squeeze as much water out from the zucchini as possible, and transfer zucchini to a large mixing bowl.
2. Add egg, flour, green onions, garlic, parsley, lemon zest, salt and black pepper. Mix to combine.
3. Heat 2 tablespoons of oil in a large nonstick skillet over medium heat.
4. Take a spoonful of the zucchini batter and flatten slightly with a spatula. Add as many as possible but without the fritters touching each other.
5. Cook fritters on both sides until crisp and golden brown, about 3 minutes on each side.
6. Transfer fritters on towel paper to drain excess oil.
7. Repeat process with remaining batter.
8. Serve with a drop of cashew sour cream or aioli.

SWEET POTATO AND BLACK BEAN VEGGIE BURGER

YIELDS 12 patties

PREP 45 minutes   COOK 45 minutes   TOTAL 1 hour, 30 minutes

Ⓝ NUT-FREE

Inspired from Mexican flavors, these flavorful baked vegetarian patties are made of sweet potatoes, brown rice, black beans and spices. You can use traditional buns and fill your burger the way you like it or skip the bread and add toppings on the patty or on the side. Serve with coleslaw or homemade baked sweet potato fries.

INGREDIENTS

1 cup water

½ cup basmati brown rice, rinsed

1 medium sweet potato, peeled and diced (about 2 cups)

1 tablespoon olive oil

1 small onion, diced

2 cloves garlic, minced

2 teaspoons ground cumin

1 teaspoon chili powder

½ teaspoon chipotle powder

1 teaspoon unrefined salt

1 can (15 ounces/425 grams) black beans, rinsed and drained

Sprouted, whole-grain or gluten-free hamburger buns

OPTIONAL TOPPINGS

Avocado or guacamole

Sliced tomatoes or pico de gallo

Sliced red onions

Lettuce

Sprouts

Condiments like ketchup, mustard, mayonnaise or hot sauce

INSTRUCTIONS

1. Start by cooking the rice. Add water to a small saucepan and bring to a boil. Add rice, reduce heat to low, cover, and simmer until rice is cooked, about 40 minutes. Fluff with a fork and set aside.
2. Preheat oven to 350F and line a large baking sheet with parchment paper. Set aside.
3. Boil or steam sweet potato until fork tender, about 10 minutes. Drain and set aside.
4. Meanwhile, in a large skillet, heat oil over medium-low heat. Add onions and garlic and cook until softened, about 3 minutes. Add cumin, chili and chipotle powder, and cook for an additional 2 minutes. Turn off heat and set aside.
5. In a food processor, combine rice, sweet potatoes, onion mixture and black beans. Pulse a few times to have your mixture stick together but do not overprocess so not to have a mushy consistency – you still want to see bits of food in the mixture for texture.
6. Scoop ¼ cup of the mixture (or more if you want bigger patties), and form patties with your hands. Place on the prepared baking sheet.
7. Bake for 40 to 45 minutes, or until the edges look slightly golden and crisp.
8. Make your burger with favorite toppings and serve with side dishes.

NOTES

To save on time, use leftover rice if you have any.
You can also use 1½ cups of freshly cooked beans.

TERIYAKI TOFU AND BROCCOLI

SERVES 4

PREP 5 minutes   COOK 30 minutes   TOTAL 35 minutes

Ⓝ NUT-FREE

This pan-fried tofu and broccoli dish tossed with a homemade teriyaki sauce makes a very satisfying vegetarian dish. Cut tofu and broccoli into small pieces, especially if serving for children, and serve over a bed of rice or noodles.

INGREDIENTS

3 tablespoons unrefined sesame oil, divided
1 head broccoli, cut into small
    florets (about 4 cups)
1 block organic tofu, firm or extra-firm
Teriyaki sauce
¼ cup gluten-free tamari
⅓ cup coconut sugar
2 tablespoons fresh lime juice
½ teaspoon ground ginger
¼ teaspoon garlic powder
Pinch red pepper flakes
1 cup water
1-2 tablespoons arrowroot or cornstarch

Cooked rice or rice noodles, for serving
1 tablespoon sesame seeds, for garnish

NOTE

For variation, you can try the dish with chicken, steak strips or shrimp instead of tofu.

INSTRUCTIONS

1. Press tofu between clean towels or paper towels to remove excess water before cooking. Cut tofu into small dices, about ¾ inch, and set aside.

2. In a large wok or pot, heat 1 tablespoon of sesame oil over medium heat. Add broccoli florets and cook until softened, about 10 minutes. Transfer broccoli to a plate and set aside.

3. In the same pot, heat 2 tablespoons of sesame oil over medium heat. Add diced tofu, in batches, if necessary, and cook until a light golden crust form on the sides, stirring occasionally to avoid sticking, about 8 to 10 minutes.

4. While tofu is cooking, make the sauce. Combine tamari, coconut sugar, lime juice, ginger, garlic, red pepper flakes and water in a small saucepan. Bring to a boil.

5. Combine 1 tablespoon of starch with 1 tablespoon of water in a small bowl and mix to combine. When the sauce starts to boil, turn off heat and whisk in starch.

6. When tofu is cooked through, add broccoli back to the pot along with all the sauce. Turn off heat, stir and let sit for about 5 minutes before serving over rice or noodles.

7. Garnish with sesame seeds.

CAULIFLOWER KUNG PAO STYLE

SERVES 4

PREP 10 minutes   COOK 25 minutes   TOTAL 35 minutes

🥜 NUT-FREE

This popular spicy Chinese dish is usually made with chicken and peanuts. This version is meat-free – using cauliflower instead of meat – and is pretty mild, which should please most children. Serve with basmati rice or quinoa, and garnish with scallions and sesame seeds. Give it a try, as it's different but very tasty!

INGREDIENTS

2 tablespoons sesame oil, coconut oil or olive oil
1 small onion, diced
2 cloves garlic, minced
1 large head cauliflower, cut into
    small florets (about 8 cups)
1 red bell pepper, seeded and diced

SAUCE

⅓ cup gluten-free tamari
⅓ cup pure maple syrup
¼ cup brown rice vinegar
1 tablespoon toasted sesame oil
1 teaspoon garlic powder
½ teaspoon ground ginger
Pinch red pepper flakes
2 tablespoons arrowroot starch, kudzu
    root or organic cornstarch
¼ cup water

Cooked basmati rice or quinoa, for serving
1 scallion, crosswise sliced, for garnish
Sesame seeds, for garnish

NOTE

For a soy-free version, use coconut
aminos instead of tamari.

INSTRUCTIONS

1. Cook rice or quinoa according to package directions.
2. Meanwhile, in a large skillet, heat oil over medium heat. Add onions and garlic, and cook until soft and fragrant, about 3 minutes.
3. Add cauliflower florets and cook until cauliflower has a golden color, stirring occasionally to avoid sticking, about 10 to 12 minutes. Then, add red bell peppers.
4. While cauliflower is cooking, make the sauce. In a small saucepan, combine tamari, maple syrup, vinegar, sesame oil, garlic powder, ground ginger and red pepper flakes. Bring to a boil.
5. Mix starch and water in a small bowl until starch is dissolved and a slurry forms. When sauce is boiling, turn off heat, add slurry and whisk to combine. Let sauce rest a few minutes to thicken.
6. Add red bell pepper and sauce to pot and cook for an additional 5 minutes. Turn off heat, stir and let rest for a couple of minutes before serving over a bed of rice or quinoa.
7. Garnish with scallions and sesame seeds if desired.

CAULIFLOWER 'ALFREDO' PASTA

SERVES 4

PREP 5 minutes   COOK 20 minutes   TOTAL 25 minutes

*The 'Alfredo' sauce in this pasta dish is made without butter, cream
or cheese. Instead, it's made with extra-virgin olive oil, cauliflower
and almond milk. It's light yet creamy and very tasty. Use your favorite
healthy pasta and add garden peas and garnish with parsley if desired.
If you are not vegetarian, you can add organic chicken strips or bacon.*

INGREDIENTS

1 package sprouted, whole-grain or
    gluten-free linguine, penne or fusilli

SAUCE

1 tablespoon extra-virgin olive oil
2 cloves garlic, minced
1 small head cauliflower, cut into florets
1 cup water
1 teaspoon unrefined salt
¼ teaspoon ground black pepper
¾ cup unsweetened plain almond milk

OPTIONAL ADD-INS & GARNISHES

¾ cup frozen peas, thawed
1 cooked chicken breast, sliced
4 slices cooked organic bacon, crumbled
Fresh parsley, minced

NOTES

Leftovers can be eaten cold as a pasta salad.
If planning to do so, use an appropriate shape
for pasta salad like penne, fusilli or macaroni.

INSTRUCTIONS

1. Bring a large pot of salted water to a boil. Add pasta and cook until pasta is al dente or to your liking. If using peas, add when pasta is a few minutes done from cooking. When pasta is cooked, drain a colander and return to pot.

2. Meanwhile, heat olive oil in a medium pot over low heat. Add garlic and cook until fragrant, about 2 minutes. Add cauliflower florets and water and bring to a boil. Cover, reduce heat to a simmer and cook until fork tender, about 10 minutes. Water should be mostly evaporated.

3. Transfer cauliflower to a blender or food processor. Add salt, black pepper and almond milk. Blend until silky smooth. Add a little more almond milk if needed.

4. Pour desired amount of sauce into the pot with pasta. Add cooked chicken strips or bacon if using. Stir to coat all the pasta and serve on plates.

5. Garnish with parsley if desired.

LOADED SWEET POTATOES

SERVES 4-6

PREP 5 minutes   COOK 45 minutes   TOTAL 50 minutes

Ⓝ NUT-FREE

Roasted sweet potatoes are loaded with a mixture of beans, corn and tomatoes and topped with your favorite toppings for a healthy, nutritious Mexican-style dish. Plan one sweet potato per person.

INGREDIENTS

4-6 medium sweet potatoes

FILLING

1 tablespoon extra-virgin olive oil

1 small onion, diced

2 cloves garlic, minced

1 jalapeño, seeded and minced

1 can (15 ounces/425 grams) black
    beans, rinsed and drained

2 ears fresh corn, kernels cut off the cob

2 Roma tomatoes, chopped

1 teaspoon chili powder

1 teaspoon ground cumin

1 teaspoon unrefined salt

    ½ lime, juiced

OPTIONAL TOPPINGS

Diced avocados or guacamole

Sour cream or cashew sour cream (page 313)

Grated Mexican cheese

Pickled jalapeños

Sliced green onions

Cilantro leaves

INSTRUCTIONS

1. Preheat oven to 400F.
2. Wash and scrub potatoes. Poke them with a fork or knife at several places, rub them with olive oil, season with salt and place them on a baking sheet. Roast until cooked through, about 45 minutes.
3. When potatoes are about halfway done from cooking, make the filling by heating olive oil over medium-low heat in a large skillet. Add onions, garlic and jalapeño, and cook until soft and fragrant, about 3 minutes. Stir in black beans, corn, tomatoes, chili powder, cumin and salt. Bring to a boil, reduce heat to low and simmer, stirring occasionally, for 10 to 15 minutes. Turn off heat, add lime juice, stir well and reserve.
4. When potatoes are done cooking, slice each potato in half lengthwise. You may wait a few minutes to let the steam out.
5. Fill the potatoes with the bean mixture and top with your favorite toppings.

LENTIL LOAF WITH OATS AND APPLES

SERVES 8

PREP 1 hour   COOK 1 hour   TOTAL 2 hours

This hearty and nutritious loaf is made with green lentils, rolled oats, apples, walnuts, raisins and thyme. It's a complete source of protein and a tremendous source of fiber and healthy fats. Serve the loaf with mashed cauliflower or potatoes and a side of green vegetables. A cranberry sauce or gravy could be made to serve with the dish as well. This loaf is ideal to serve during winter or the holidays. Leftovers can be frozen.

INGREDIENTS

1 cup green lentils, rinsed

2¼ cup low-sodium vegetable broth or water

2 tablespoons extra-virgin olive oil

1 medium onion, diced

4 cloves garlic, minced

1 cup diced carrots

1 cup diced celery

1 large apple, cored and diced

2 teaspoons unrefined salt, divided

1 teaspoon dried thyme

¼ teaspoon red pepper flakes

¾ cup gluten-free rolled oats

¾ cup walnuts

¼ cup raisins

3 tablespoons ground flaxseeds

GLAZE

¼ cup tomato paste

2 tablespoons balsamic vinegar

2 tablespoons maple syrup

Pinch smoked paprika

Pinch unrefined salt

INSTRUCTIONS

1. Bring broth or water in a saucepan to a boil. Add lentils, cover, bring heat to low and simmer until liquid has been absorbed and lentils are tender, about 30 to 40 minutes. Turn off heat, give the lentils a stir and set aside.

2. Preheat oven to 350F and line a loaf pan with parchment paper. Set aside.

3. In a large skillet, heat olive oil over medium-low heat. Add onions and garlic and cook until softened, about 3 minutes. Add 1 teaspoon of salt and carrots, celery, apples, thyme and red pepper flakes, and cook until vegetables are tender, about 10 minutes, stirring often. Set aside to cool.

4. Put lentils in a food processor along with the vegetable mixture.

5. Add oats, walnuts, raisins and flaxseeds and 1 teaspoon of salt. Pulse several times for a few seconds to break down the mixture but without over processing. You want chunks of lentils and vegetables intact in the loaf for texture.

6. Place mixture into the prepared loaf pan and press firmly and evenly with your hands or spatula.

7. In a small bowl, mix the tomato paste with the balsamic vinegar, maple syrup, paprika and salt, and spread evenly on top of the loaf.

8. Bake for 50 to 60 minutes or until the edges start to look darker. Rest loaf 10 to 15 minutes before removing from pan and slicing.

NOTES

To save on time, cook lentils ahead of time or make the loaf a day in advance and refrigerate until ready to cook. The loaf freezes well. Slice individual pieces and store accordingly.

GARLIC ROASTED
BROCCOLI
SEE PAGE 225

MASHED
CAULIFLOWER
SEE PAGE 228

RATATOUILLE

SERVES 6

PREP 15 minutes   COOK 1 hour, 15 minutes   TOTAL 1 hour, 30 minutes

🥜 NUT-FREE

Ratatouille is a French stewed vegetable dish made with fresh vegetables. It's best made during summer when vegetables are at peak freshness. It's a tasty, nutritious dish full of colors and flavors. It's delicious as is or served with grilled chicken, lamb or fish, poached egg, pasta, couscous, quinoa or polenta. Enjoy warm or cold or at room temperature.

INGREDIENTS

2 tablespoons olive oil, divided
1 large yellow onion, diced
2 bell peppers, diced
2 medium zucchinis, diced
1 large eggplant, cut into bite-sized cubes
4 cloves garlic, minced
2 large organic ripe tomatoes, diced
1 bay leaf
4 sprigs thyme
1 teaspoon unrefined salt, plus
    more for seasoning
¼ teaspoon ground black pepper
¼ teaspoon red pepper flakes
¼ cup loosely packed basil, minced (optional)

INSTRUCTIONS

1. In a large Dutch oven or pot, heat 1 tablespoon of olive oil over medium heat.
2. Add onions and sauté until onions are soft and fragrant, about 3 minutes.
3. Add bell peppers and zucchini, and a pinch of salt, and sauté until vegetables have softened, about 3 more minutes.
4. Transfer vegetables to a large bowl. Set aside.
5. Deglaze pan if needed with a little water and turn heat to medium-low.
6. Add eggplant and a pinch of salt and cook until softened, about 10 minutes. Transfer eggplant to the bowl with the other vegetables.
7. Add 1 tablespoon of olive oil and sauté garlic until fragrant, about 30 seconds.
8. Add tomatoes, bay leaf, thyme, red pepper flakes, salt and black pepper. Stir and let cook for about 2 minutes.
9. With a slotted spoon, add cooked vegetables back to the pot, avoiding adding liquid from the bottom of the bowl.
10. Bring pot to a simmer and cook until vegetables have achieved the desired consistency you like. It can be ready almost right away if you like vegetables a little chunkier or up to an hour if you like them softer. If cooking longer, stir often to avoid sticking at the bottom of the pan.
11. Turn off heat, remove bay leaf and thyme sprigs. Stir in fresh basil and mix to combine.
12. Serve ratatouille warm or at room temperature. Refrigerate any leftovers.

NOTES

You can also replace a zucchini with a summer squash, if you'd like.

HEALTHY 'MAC N' CHEESE'

SERVES 2-4

PREP 5 minutes   COOK 15 minutes   TOTAL 20 minutes

This guilt-free macaroni and cheese recipe is made with gluten-free pasta and a sauce made of cashews, coconut milk and nutritional yeast. Carrots are added to give the sauce its orange color. It's healthy but comforting and satisfying. Give it a try — you will be surprised how close it is to traditional mac and cheese. For small children, you may also try using a fun pasta shape!

INGREDIENTS

1 package gluten-free pasta like chickpea, quinoa or brown rice
1 cup raw cashews, soaked in water for 1 to 4 hours
½ to ¾ cup water
¼ cup full-fat canned coconut milk
¼ cup nutritional yeast
½ cup sliced carrots
1 garlic clove
1 tablespoon fresh lemon juice
1 teaspoon unrefined salt
Pinch ground black pepper

INSTRUCTIONS

1. Cook pasta in a pot of salted boiling water until al dente or cooked to your liking. Drain in a colander and return to pot.
2. Meanwhile, make the sauce: First, drain cashews in a colander and rinse under running water. Then, add cashews, water, coconut milk, nutritional yeast, carrots, garlic, lemon juice, salt and black pepper in a blender and blend until silky smooth. Start with ½ cup water and increase if needed.
3. Pour sauce into pot with cooked pasta, stir to combine and serve.

SPINACH TOFU LASAGNA

SERVES 8

PREP 45 minutes   COOK 50 minutes   TOTAL 1 hour, 35 minutes

Ⓝ NUT-FREE

This vegan lasagna is made with a flavorful and easy-to-make marinara, and a delectable spinach tofu 'ricotta' – no real cheese needed. Frozen spinach is used in the recipe as it's more economical and convenient. Thaw spinach before chopping and adding it to the ricotta. The sauce and ricotta can be made ahead of time as can the lasagna itself. After putting it together, refrigerate and bake when ready to use.

INGREDIENTS

Marinara sauce, recipe below
Tofu 'ricotta,' recipe below
1 bag (8 ounces/227 grams)
    frozen spinach, thawed
1 package brown rice lasagna noodles
Nutritional yeast, for topping
Dried oregano, for topping

MARINARA SAUCE

2 tablespoons extra-virgin olive oil
1 medium yellow onion, chopped
2 large cloves garlic, minced
1 medium carrot, peeled and finely chopped
1 teaspoon dried oregano
Pinch red pepper flakes
1 can (28 ounces/794 grams) whole peeled
    tomatoes, preferably San Marzano
1 teaspoon unrefined salt
Freshly ground black pepper

TOFU 'RICOTTA'

1 block (16 ounces/454 grams) organic
    tofu, firm or extra-firm
3 tablespoons nutritional yeast
2 tablespoons fresh lemon juice
2 teaspoons dried oregano
½ teaspoon dried basil
½ teaspoon garlic powder
1 teaspoon unrefined salt
Freshly ground black pepper
4 tablespoons extra-virgin olive oil

INSTRUCTIONS

1. Start by making the sauce. Heat olive oil in a small saucepan over medium-low heat. Add onions, carrots and garlic and cook until onions start to soften, about 3 minutes. Add oregano and red pepper flakes, and cook until onions are very soft, about 7 to 10 more minutes. Add tomatoes and season with salt and black pepper. Bring to a boil. Reduce heat to low and simmer for 30 to 60 minutes. Allow to cool. Blend carefully until smooth and set aside.

2. While sauce is simmering, make tofu 'ricotta.' Press tofu between kitchen or paper towels to remove excess water. Chop tofu and add it to a high-speed blender. Add nutritional yeast, lemon juice, oregano, basil, garlic, salt, black pepper and olive oil. At low speed, blend until mostly smooth, scraping down sides as needed. Transfer to a medium mixing bowl.

3. Put thawed spinach between kitchen towels and press to remove excess water. Then, chop spinach finely and add to ricotta mixture. Mix to combine and set aside.

4. Preheat oven to 375F.

5. Bring a large pot of water to a boil. Salt water, add lasagna noodles, and cook until al dente, about 8 to 10 minutes. Drain in a colander and set aside.

6. Lay a thin layer of sauce at the bottom of a lasagna pan. Add a single layer of noodles. Distribute about half the 'ricotta' evenly on the layer of noodles. Add a layer of sauce and another layer of noodles. Then, repeat process until you get to last layer of noodles. Then, add a thin layer of sauce and sprinkle with nutritional yeast and dried oregano.

7. Cover lasagna with foil and bake for 30 minutes. Then, uncover and bake for another 20 minutes.

8. Allow to cool for 5 to 10 minutes before slicing and serving.

NOTES

- Substitute spinach for kale if you prefer. You won't notice the difference in taste, and it's a terrific way to have your family eat this nutritious, leafy green vegetable.
- If you don't mind gluten-free pasta, substitute with your favorite lasagna noodles.

TEMPEH WITH PEANUT SAUCE AND KALE

SERVES 2-4

PREP 5 minutes   COOK 20 minutes   TOTAL 25 minutes

If you haven't had tempeh yet, it's an excellent recipe to start with. It's flavorful, creamy and satisfying, and the sauce is seriously addictive. Leftover sauce can even be used as a dip for roasted vegetables or diced tofu. Serve the dish over basmati rice or cauliflower rice.

INGREDIENTS

2 tablespoons sesame oil, peanut
    oil or coconut oil
1 package tempeh, cubed
1 cup chopped kale, fresh or frozen
1 cup peanut butter sauce, recipe below
Cooked rice or cauliflower rice, for serving

SAUCE

1 can (13.5 ounces/400 millimeters)
    full-fat coconut milk
½ cup creamy peanut butter
1 lime, juiced
2 tablespoons organic honey
    or pure maple syrup
2 tablespoons gluten-free tamari
    or coconut aminos
½ teaspoon garlic powder
¼ teaspoon ground ginger
¼ teaspoon red pepper flakes
¼ teaspoon unrefined salt

INSTRUCTIONS

1. Make the sauce by blending the coconut milk with peanut butter, lime juice, honey, tamari, garlic, ginger, red pepper flakes and salt. Set aside.

2. In a large pot or deep skillet, heat oil over medium heat. Add tempeh and fry on both sides until golden in color, about 3 minutes on each side.

3. Add kale and 1 cup of sauce. Reduce heat to low and cook until tempeh is warmed through, about 8 to 10 minutes.

4. Serve over rice.

NOTE

You can substitute spinach or chopped broccoli for the kale if you prefer.

SPAGHETTI WITH AVOCADO BASIL SAUCE

SERVES 4

PREP 5 minutes   COOK 15 minutes   TOTAL 20 minutes

Ⓝ NUT-FREE

This creamy, raw avocado basil sauce is tossed with spaghetti and halved cherry tomatoes for a light and nutritious pasta dish. For extra proteins, add chicken strips, sea scallops or shrimp. For a grain-free option, use zucchini noodles.

INGREDIENTS

1 package sprouted, whole-grain or gluten-free spaghetti, or zucchini noodles
1 cup cherry tomatoes, halves
Freshly ground black pepper, for garnish

SAUCE

1 large ripe avocado, peeled and pitted
1 tablespoon extra-virgin olive oil
1 tablespoon fresh lemon juice
¾ teaspoon unrefined salt
¼ teaspoon ground black pepper
1 small clove garlic, minced
¼ cup loosely packed fresh basil leaves, plus more for garnish
⅓ cup water

INSTRUCTIONS

1. Cook pasta in a large pot of salted boiling water until al dente. Drain in a colander, put pasta back into the pot and stir in halved tomatoes.
2. While pasta is cooking, make the sauce. Put the avocado, olive oil, lemon juice, salt, black pepper, garlic, basil and water in a small blender and purée until smooth.
3. Add desired amount of sauce into the pot and stir to combine.
4. Divide between plates, and garnish with fresh basil and ground black pepper, if desired.

NOTES

To make zucchini noodles, use a spiralizer. Otherwise, you can sometimes find them already made in grocery stores in the refrigerated section. Cook the zucchini noodles slightly in a pan with a little olive oil before adding the sauce. Plan one zucchini per person.

SIDE DISHES

If you or your family don't enjoy eating cruciferous or root vegetables, you may change your mind after trying the following recipes. These dishes offer a distinctive yet fun and tasty way to incorporate them into your diet.

GARLICKY GREEN BEANS

SERVES 4

PREP 2 minutes   COOK 8 minutes   TOTAL 10 minutes

Ⓝ NUT-FREE

Fresh green beans cooked in a skillet with olive oil, garlic, red pepper flakes, salt and pepper make for a healthy, flavorful side dish.

INGREDIENTS

¾ pound green beans, ends trimmed
2 tablespoons extra-virgin olive oil or grass-fed butter
1 large garlic clove, minced
Pinch red pepper flakes
Unrefined salt
Freshly ground black pepper

INSTRUCTIONS

1. Blanch the green beans by bringing a large pot of salted water to a boil. Add green beans and cook until bright green in color and tender-crisp, about 2 minutes. Drain in a colander.
2. In a large skillet, heat oil or butter over medium heat. Add garlic and cook until fragrant, about 30 seconds.
3. Add green beans and red pepper flakes, and season with salt and black pepper.
4. Cook until beans are tender, about 5 minutes and serve.

CAULIFLOWER BRUSSELS SPROUTS CASSEROLE WITH BACON

SERVES 4-6

PREP 25 minutes   COOK 25 minutes   TOTAL 50 minutes

Ⓢ NUT-FREE

This is a distinctive side dish perfect for fall and winter or the holidays. It's warm, creamy and satisfying. Bacon adds a delicious smoky flavor to the dish. It's always best to choose organic or turkey bacon. If making for vegetarians, simply omit or use eggplant or coconut 'bacon.'

INGREDIENTS

4 cups cauliflower florets, from about
    1 medium or large cauliflower
2 cups sliced Brussels sprouts
3 tablespoons extra-virgin olive oil, divided
1 small onion, diced
2 cloves garlic, minced
1 package (8-10 ounces) organic bacon or
    turkey bacon, cut into small pieces

2 tablespoons coconut flour
1 can (13.5 ounces/400 milliliters)
    full-fat coconut milk
¾ teaspoon unrefined salt
¼ teaspoon ground black pepper
⅛ teaspoon ground nutmeg

INSTRUCTIONS

1. Preheat oven to 400F.
2. Cook cauliflower and Brussels sprouts in a large pot of salted boiling water until tender, about 5 minutes. Drain in a colander for a few minutes.
3. Heat 1 tablespoon of olive oil over medium-low heat. Add onions and garlic and cook until very soft, about 5 minutes. Transfer to a large baking dish and set aside.
4. In the same skillet, cook bacon until crispy. Transfer to paper towels to absorb excess fat. Reserve.
5. Add 2 tablespoons of olive oil in a small saucepan over medium-low heat. Whisk in coconut flour and cook for 1 minute. Whisk in all the coconut milk slowly. Bring to a boil, reduce heat to low and simmer until thickened, about 10 minutes. Turn off heat and season with salt, black pepper and nutmeg.
6. Transfer cauliflower and Brussels sprouts to the baking dish along with the onions and garlic and pour all the sauce. Top with bacon.
7. Bake until some of the vegetables start to get crisp, about 25 minutes. Serve warm.

NOTE

For a vegetarian dish, simply omit bacon.

GARLIC ROASTED BROCCOLI

SERVES 4

PREP 5 minutes   COOK 20 minutes   TOTAL 25 minutes

(●) NUT-FREE

This is a flavorful and healthy vegetable side dish for families. Delicious served with a dip as well.

INGREDIENTS

1 bunch broccoli, cut into florets
2 tablespoons olive oil
1 clove garlic, minced
¼ teaspoon unrefined salt
Pinch red pepper flakes

INSTRUCTIONS

1. Preheat oven to 400F.
2. Combine broccoli, olive oil, garlic, salt and red pepper flakes in a large bowl and mix to combine.
3. Place on a large baking sheet, making sure the broccoli florets are not touching each other.
4. Roast until crisp, about 15 to 20 minutes.

HONEY-ROASTED SPICED CARROTS

SERVES 4

PREP 5 minutes   COOK 25 minutes   TOTAL 30 minutes

Ⓢ NUT-FREE

Incredibly nutritious, this side dish is flavorful, slightly sweet and comforting. This is a perfect side dish for grilled fish or meat, tofu and couscous or to add to Buddha bowls.

INGREDIENTS

8 medium carrots, peeled and tops trimmed, about 1 pound
1 tablespoon olive oil
1 tablespoon local honey
½ teaspoon unrefined salt
¼ teaspoon ground cumin
¼ teaspoon ground coriander
¼ teaspoon garlic powder
¼ teaspoon paprika
¼ teaspoon ground black pepper
Minced parsley, to garnish (optional)

INSTRUCTIONS

1. Preheat oven to 400F and line a large baking sheet with parchment paper. Set aside.
2. Peel carrots and cut them in half and then in half lengthwise. If you prefer, slice them in half lengthwise.
3. Add them to a large mixing bowl and add olive oil, honey, salt, cumin, coriander, garlic, paprika, salt and black pepper. Toss to combine.
4. Spread carrots onto the prepared baking sheet in a single layer, making sure they don't touch each other.
5. Place into oven and cook until tender and caramelized, about 35 to 40 minutes.
6. Garnish with minced parsley if desired and serve.

NOTE

For a more colorful dish, use rainbow carrots.

MASHED CAULIFLOWER

SERVES 2-4

PREP 5 minutes   COOK 15 minutes   TOTAL 20 minutes

Ⓝ NUT-FREE

Mashed cauliflower is similar to mashed potatoes but lighter and healthier. It's lower in carbohydrates, easier to make and still very creamy and tasty. Give the recipe a try – you will be amazed. Plus, it's a very enjoyable way to encourage your children to eat cauliflower.

INGREDIENTS

1 medium cauliflower, cut into florets (about 4 cups)
2 tablespoons grass-fed butter or extra-virgin olive oil
½ teaspoon unrefined salt
Freshly ground black pepper
¼ teaspoon garlic powder (optional)

INSTRUCTIONS

1. Steam or boil cauliflower florets in a large pot of salted water until soft tender but not mushy, about 15 minutes. Drain in a colander.
2. Transfer cauliflower to a food processor. Add butter or oil, salt, black pepper, and garlic powder if using.
3. Process until smooth, scraping down the side with a silicone spatula as needed.
4. Serve with your main course.

NOTE

If you don't have a food processor, you can mash the cauliflower with a fork or a potato masher, but it will be chunkier.

ROASTED MAPLE BRUSSELS SPROUTS

SERVES 2-4

PREP 1 minutes   COOK 30 minutes   TOTAL 40 minutes

Ⓝ NUT-FREE

Roasting Brussels sprouts is one of the best ways to serve your family this cruciferous vegetable. They caramelize as they roast and, as a result, become crisp on the outside, tender on the inside and slightly sweet. They make a perfect side dish for fall and winter.

INGREDIENTS

1 pound Brussels sprouts, trimmed, outer leaves removed and cut in half lengthwise

2 tablespoons olive oil

2 tablespoon pure maple syrup

1 tablespoon balsamic vinegar

½ teaspoon unrefined salt

¼ teaspoon ground black pepper

INSTRUCTIONS

1. Preheat oven to 425F, and line a large baking sheet with parchment paper. Set aside.
2. Trim stem ends off Brussels sprouts, remove outer leaves and cut them in half lengthwise.
3. Put Brussels sprouts in a mixing bowl and toss with olive oil, maple syrup, balsamic vinegar and salt and black pepper.
4. Spread Brussels sprouts onto the baking sheet in a single layer.
5. Roast until tender and crispy, about 25 to 30 minutes.

NOTE

For a more festive dish, add cranberries and toasted pecans, walnuts or almonds once the Brussels sprouts are done cooking.

CRISPY BAKED SWEET POTATO FRIES

SERVES 4

PREP 10 minutes   COOK 30 minutes   TOTAL 40 minutes

Ⓝ NUT-FREE

The secret to making crispy baked sweet potato fries is not to overcrowd the pan, bake at a high temperature and season immediately with salt after cooking. The result? Crispy, satisfying sweet potato fries. Serve with homemade ketchup or mayonnaise if desired.

INGREDIENTS

2 sweet potatoes, about 1½ pounds
4 teaspoons potato starch (or tapioca or organic cornstarch)
2 tablespoons olive oil
Unrefined salt, to taste
½ teaspoon smoked paprika, chipotle powder or garlic powder (optional)

INSTRUCTIONS

1. Preheat oven to 425F.
2. Set two large nonstick baking sheets aside. Alternatively, line two half sheet pans with aluminum foil and lightly spray the pans with oil to avoid sticking. Set aside.
3. Peel sweet potatoes and cut in ¼-inch sticks.
4. Put fries in a large plastic bag, add starch, seal bag and shake vigorously to coat all the fries.
5. Add oil to the bag and spices, if using, and toss to coat. You can also toss everything in a mixing bowl.
6. Arrange fries in a single layer on the baking sheets, making sure they don't touch each other.
7. Bake for about 30 minutes. Halfway through the baking time, flip the fries with a spatula, and then alternate the positions of the baking sheets on the top and bottom racks in the oven.
8. Remove from oven, let cool for a few minutes and sprinkle with salt to taste.

NOTE

If you rather not use starch, simply omit. It will still work well, but just won't get as crispy.

SNACKS AND DIPS

For children, raw vegetables are almost always enjoyed better with a dip! In the next pages, you will find six healthy and easy-to-make dips to serve with vegetables, tofu, meat or healthy crackers, as well as a couple crunchy snacks. The dips can even be served as spreads for sandwiches.

BABA GANOUSH

SERVES 4

PREP 15 minutes   COOK 45 minutes   TOTAL 1 hour

🥜 NUT-FREE

Don't be intimidated—Baba Ganoush is very easy to make. Plus, it's absolutely delicious, especially when combined with pita bread or pita chips, roasted vegetables or grilled meat. It's also a great party dip, so give it a try — you won't be disappointed!

INGREDIENTS

1 large eggplant
¼ cup tahini
1 garlic clove, minced
¼ cup fresh lemon juice
¼ teaspoon ground cumin
½ teaspoon unrefined salt

INSTRUCTIONS

1. Preheat oven to 375F.
2. Prick the eggplant with a fork in several places and place on a baking sheet.
3. Roast until very soft, about 45 minutes.
4. Remove from oven, let it cool and peel off the skin.
5. Put the flesh of the eggplant into a mixing bowl and mash it with a fork until smooth.
6. Add tahini, garlic, lemon juice, cumin and salt. Mix well and pour into a serving bowl.
7. Serve at room temperature.

CASHEW 'RANCH'

SERVES 4

PREP 5 minutes   TOTAL 5 minutes

You won't be missing your traditional ranch here. This sauce is divine. It's not only a delicious sauce but a nutritious one too. Use it as a dip or to add in salads, veggie burgers or to serve with chicken tenders or zucchini fritters.

INGREDIENTS

1 cup raw cashews
½ to ¾ cup water
¼ cup avocado oil or extra-virgin olive oil
1 lemon, juiced
½ teaspoon garlic powder
½ teaspoon onion powder
½ teaspoon dried dill
½ teaspoon parsley flakes
1 teaspoon unrefined salt
½ teaspoon ground black pepper

INSTRUCTIONS

1. Place cashews in a bowl and fill with water. Let soak on the counter for 2 to 4 hours. Drain and rinse cashews.
2. Place cashews in a blender along with ½ cup water, oil, lemon juice, garlic powder, onion powder, dill, parsley, salt and black pepper.
3. Blend until smooth, scraping down the sides of the blender with a spatula as needed. Add a little more water if necessary.
4. Serve immediately or refrigerate until ready to use.

ASIAN-INSPIRED
PEANUT BUTTER

CASHEW
RANCH

CHUNKY
GUACAMOLE

QUICK
HUMMUS

TZATZIKI
SAUCE

BABA
GANOUSH

TZATZIKI SAUCE

SERVES 4

PREP 10 minutes   TOTAL 10 minutes

Ⓝ NUT-FREE OPTION

This sauce is creamy, light, refreshing and very tasty. It's made with plain full-fat yogurt, but a plain, dairy-free yogurt can be used for a dairy-free option. Serve it with crudités, roasted vegetables, baked pita chips or grilled meat or fish.

INGREDIENTS

½ English cucumber
1 cup organic Greek yogurt (cow, goat or sheep or plain dairy-free yogurt)
1 tablespoon fresh mint, minced
1 tablespoon fresh dill, minced
1 tablespoon fresh lemon juice
1 small clove garlic, minced
⅛ teaspoon unrefined salt
Freshly ground black pepper

INSTRUCTIONS

1. Peel the cucumber, slice it in half lengthwise, scrape out seeds with a spoon and grate it. Then, remove excess water by squeezing the grated cucumber with your hands using a kitchen towel or paper towel over the sink or a bowl. Then, place cucumber in a medium mixing bowl.
2. Add yogurt, mint, dill, lemon juice, garlic, salt and black pepper to bowl with the cucumber. Stir to combine.
3. Refrigerate until ready to use.

NOTE

Mint can be omitted if you dislike it or don't have it available; however, it adds a very refreshing taste to tzatziki sauce.

QUICK HUMMUS

SERVES 4

PREP 15 minutes   TOTAL 15 minutes

🥜 NUT-FREE

Although the best hummus is made from dried chickpeas, this hummus recipe is very convenient as it's made with canned chickpeas. It's quick and easy to make yet very creamy and just as delicious. Use it as a dip for crudités or pita chips, eat with falafels or pita bread or use it to make sandwiches.

INGREDIENTS

1 can (15 ounces/425 grams) chickpeas, rinsed and drained
½ cup tahini
¼ cup fresh lemon juice
1 small clove garlic, finely chopped
½ teaspoon ground cumin
¾ teaspoon unrefined salt
½ cup filtered water

OPTIONAL GARNISHES
Extra-virgin olive oil
Paprika
Fresh parsley, minced

INSTRUCTIONS

1. Optional but recommended step: Place rinsed and drained chickpeas between two kitchen towels and rub with your hands to remove all the loose chickpea skins as possible. Discard skins. This step makes the hummus even creamier and tastier.
2. Add chickpeas, tahini, lemon juice, garlic, cumin and salt in a food processor. Process until smooth, scraping sides and bottom of the bowl with a spatula. While processing, add water slowly and process until very smooth.
3. Transfer hummus to a bowl and, if desired, drizzle with extra-virgin olive oil, sprinkle with paprika and garnish with fresh parsley.

CHUNKY GUACAMOLE

SERVES 2

PREP 5 minutes   TOTAL 5 minutes

Ⓝ NUT-FREE

This is a flavorful chunky guacamole made with avocado, tomatoes, scallions and cilantro. Double the recipe if needed.

INGREDIENTS

1 large or 2 small avocados, pitted

2 tablespoons diced organic tomatoes

1 scallion, thinly sliced

1 tablespoon fresh lime juice

1 teaspoon extra-virgin olive oil

1 teaspoon cilantro, leaves only, minced

⅛ teaspoon unrefined salt

Freshly ground black pepper

INSTRUCTIONS

1. In a small bowl, mash avocado with a fork.
2. Stir in tomatoes, scallion, lime juice, olive oil, cilantro, salt and black pepper.
3. Serve immediately.

NOTE

Guacamole can be made ahead of time. Store it in an airtight container and, to avoid oxidation, add a small amount of water on top of the guacamole but do not mix it in. When ready to use, pour off the water.

ASIAN-INSPIRED PEANUT BUTTER

SERVES 2-4

PREP 5 minutes   TOTAL 5 minutes

Ⓝ NUT-FREE

This Asian-inspired peanut butter sauce is deliciously addictive. It's creamy, sweet and salty. Serve it as a dip for crudités, roasted vegetables, tofu or tempeh chunks, Buddha bowls, spring rolls, tandoori grilled chicken or as a sauce to drizzle on top of Asian dishes. If making as a sauce, make it thinner by adding a little more water or coconut milk.

INGREDIENTS

¼ cup creamy peanut butter, preferably organic or freshly made

1 lime, juiced

1 tablespoon raw honey or pure maple syrup

1 tablespoon gluten-free tamari

½ teaspoon garlic powder

¼ teaspoon ground ginger

Pinch red pepper flakes

2-4 tablespoons water or full-fat coconut milk

1 tablespoon nutritional yeast (optional)

INSTRUCTIONS

1. Put peanut butter, lime juice, honey, nutritional yeast, if using, tamari, garlic, ginger, red pepper flakes and 2 tablespoons of water or coconut milk in a small blender and blend until smooth. Add a tablespoon of water or coconut milk, one tablespoon at the time, until desired consistency.

2. Serve or store in a small container in the refrigerator until ready to use.

EASY KALE CHIPS

SERVES 2-4

PREP 10 minutes   COOK 40 minutes   TOTAL 50 minutes

Ⓝ NUT-FREE

Once upon a time, I was a raw foodist and vegan and used my dehydrator to make many delicious raw foods, including kale chips. This recipe is more convenient, especially for busy people, as it uses the oven instead of the dehydrator, so it cooks faster.

INGREDIENTS

1 bunch kale, stemmed, washed and dried
2 tablespoons extra-virgin olive oil
⅛ teaspoon unrefined salt

FOR CHEESY FLAVOR, ADD:
2 tablespoons nutritional yeast

OPTIONAL ADD-IN SPICES
¼ teaspoon smoked paprika
¼ teaspoon garlic powder

INSTRUCTIONS

1. Preheat oven to 300F and line 2 large baking sheets with parchment paper. Set aside.
2. Tear kale into bite-sized pieces and put into a large mixing bowl.
3. Stir in olive oil and salt as well as nutritional yeast, smoked paprika and garlic powder, if using. Mix to combine.
4. Place the leaves in a single layer on the baking sheets.
5. Bake for 40 minutes, turning kale every 10 minutes.

NOTE

Make sure the kale is very dry; otherwise, the leaves will be a little soggy.

ROASTED CHICKPEAS

SERVES 2-4

PREP 10 minutes   COOK 30 minutes   TOTAL 40 minutes

Ⓝ NUT-FREE

Roasted chickpeas make a wonderful snack for children and adults. Because they are small and crunchy, infants and babies should not eat them. They are delicious eaten on their own, but they are also great added to salads or to garnish soups. They are best eaten the same day.

INGREDIENTS

1 can (15 ounces/425 grams) organic chickpeas, rinsed and drained
1 tablespoon extra-virgin olive oil
½ teaspoon unrefined salt

FOR CHILI LIME FLAVOR, ADD:

1-1½ teaspoon chili powder
1 teaspoon lime zest

FOR CURRY FLAVOR, ADD:

1 teaspoon curry powder

FOR BARBECUE FLAVOR, ADD:

1 teaspoon coconut sugar
1 teaspoon smoked paprika
½ teaspoon chili powder
½ teaspoon garlic powder
½ teaspoon onion powder
¼ teaspoon ground black pepper

INSTRUCTIONS

1. Preheat oven to 400F and line a large baking sheet with parchment paper. Set aside.
2. Pat drained chickpeas dry with a kitchen towel or paper towel to remove excess water. Remove any loose skins.
3. In a large mixing bowl, combine chickpeas, oil and salt, and toss to combine.
4. Spread chickpeas in a single layer on baking sheet.
5. Roast until crispy, about 30 minutes, shaking the pan every 10 minutes.
6. Add extra seasonings if desired, stir and serve, or allow the chickpeas to cool before storing into a container.

DESSERTS

These flourless and healthy no-bake dessert recipes, which also make nutritious snacks, are made with natural, high-quality ingredients and are light, tasty and easy to make.

You will find recipes like applesauce, banana ice cream, raspberry sorbet, fruit gummies, Jell-O, rice pudding and raw bars. They are gluten- and dairy-free, and most of them are grain- and nut-free as well.

AVOCADO CHOCOLATE PUDDING

SERVES 1-2

PREP 5 minutes   TOTAL 5 minutes

Ⓝ NUT-FREE

*This creamy chocolate pudding made with avocado,
coconut oil, honey and cacao is seriously addictive.
Serve it as a healthy snack or dessert.*

INGREDIENTS

½ cup filtered water
1 large ripe avocado
1 tablespoon coconut oil
¼ cup organic honey, or pure maple syrup
⅓ cup raw cacao powder
Pinch Himalayan salt

OPTIONAL TOPPINGS
Chopped hazelnuts
Chopped dark chocolate
Fleur de sel

INSTRUCTIONS

1. Place water, avocado, coconut oil, honey, cacao powder and salt in a blender and slowly blend until smooth. You may need to scrape down the side with a spatula.
2. Transfer to a bowl and garnish with toppings if desired.
3. Enjoy immediately or store in the refrigerator. Eat within the same day.

RASPBERRY
SORBET

BANANA ICE CREAM

SERVES 2-4

PREP 15 minutes   TOTAL 15 minutes

⊘ NUT-FREE

If you haven't made banana ice cream yet, it's time to try! It's cold, smooth and creamy, and naturally sweet – no refined sugar, milk, cream or eggs in this recipe. It's an absolute guilt-free ice cream. Top with your favorite healthy toppings if desired.

INGREDIENTS

4 frozen ripe bananas, peeled
    and cut into chunks
2 tablespoons pure maple syrup
½ teaspoon nonalcoholic vanilla extract

OPTIONAL TOPPINGS
Berries
Coconut whipped cream
Dark chocolate chips or chocolate sauce

INSTRUCTIONS

1. Put chunks of banana into a container or resealable plastic bag and freeze overnight.
2. When ready to use, take the bananas out of the refrigerator and let them sit at room temperature for 5 to 10 minutes to soften them up.
3. Add to food processor with maple syrup and vanilla. Process, scraping down sides with a silicone spatula as needed, until very smooth.
4. Pour into bowls, add your favorite toppings if desired, and serve soft immediately or store in the freezer to enjoy later.

NOTE

To have the most naturally sweet banana ice cream possible, start with very ripe bananas, preferably with brown spots on them.

RASPBERRY SORBET

SERVES 2-4

PREP 10 minutes   TOTAL 10 minutes

Ⓝ NUT-FREE

This refreshing raspberry sorbet is made with three ingredients only. It's easy to make and makes a lovely afternoon snack or dessert. Enjoy with a scoop of banana ice cream if you like for a special treat.

INGREDIENTS

2 cups frozen raspberries
2 tablespoons pure maple syrup
1 teaspoon fresh lemon juice

INSTRUCTIONS

1. Put frozen raspberries in a food processor and allow to thaw slightly, about 8 to 10 minutes.
2. Add maple syrup and lemon juice and process until mostly smooth, scraping down sides as needed. It's normal to see raspberry seeds in the sorbet.
3. Enjoy immediately or transfer to a container and freeze until ready to use.

NO-BAKE GOJI AND DARK CHOCOLATE BARS

YIELDS 10-15 bars

PREP 15 minutes   TOTAL 15 minutes plus chill time

These granola bars are not baked which means that all the nutrients are preserved. They definitely have a different mouthfeel than regular granola bars but they taste just as good, if not better. You will be surprised by how flavorful and satisfying they are. These bars make a perfect after school snack.

INGREDIENTS

2¼ cup gluten-free rolled oats
1 cup slivered almonds
½ cup creamy almond butter
¼ cup goji berries
⅓ cup raw or local honey
⅓ cup coconut oil

1 teaspoon nonalcoholic vanilla extract
½ teaspoon ground cinnamon
¼ teaspoon unrefined salt
1 extra dark chocolate bar (3.5 ounces/100 grams), finely chopped

INSTRUCTIONS

1. Oil an 8x8-inch pan lightly with coconut oil, and line with parchment paper. Set aside.
2. Put oats, almonds, almond butter, goji berries, honey, coconut oil, vanilla, cinnamon, salt, and chocolate into a food processor, and process until well-combined, scraping down sides as needed with a silicone spatula.
3. Put batter into prepared cake pan and press firmly and evenly.
4. Store in the refrigerator for at least 2 hours.
5. Remove from pan and slice into bars.
6. Put bars into a container and store in the refrigerator.

NOTES

You can use a little more or less chocolate if you prefer.
I personally like to use 85 percent dark chocolate.

COCONUT PEANUT BUTTER BALLS

YIELDS 24 balls

PREP 10 minutes   TOTAL 10 minutes plus chill time

These little no-bake treats are perfect for hungry little tummies. Made with coconut flakes, peanut butter, local honey and coconut oil, they are very nutritious. Raw cacao is optional but recommended as it improves taste and provides magnesium and antioxidants. For a caffeine-free treat, use carob powder.

INGREDIENTS

2 cups unsweetened coconut flakes
½ cup creamy peanut butter or almond butter
¼ cup local honey or pure maple syrup
2 tablespoons coconut oil
⅛ teaspoon unrefined salt
2 tablespoons organic raw cacao or carob powder (optional)
Coconut flakes, for rolling (optional)

INSTRUCTIONS

1. Line a baking sheet with parchment paper. Set aside.
2. Put coconut flakes, peanut butter, honey, coconut oil and salt, and cacao powder, if using, into your food processor and process until combined, about 10 to 15 seconds.
3. Scoop about 1 tablespoon of batter and form into balls with your hands.
4. Roll them in coconut flakes if desired.
5. Place them on a cookie sheet and refrigerate until set. They can also be frozen.

COCONUT WHIPPED CREAM WITH BERRIES

SERVES 2

PREP 10 minutes   TOTAL 10 minutes

Ⓝ NUT-FREE

This homemade coconut whipped cream is mixed with fresh berries for a light and refreshing dessert.

INGREDIENTS

1 can (13.5 ounces/400 milliliters)
full-fat coconut milk, refrigerated

1 tablespoon pure maple syrup
½ teaspoon nonalcoholic vanilla extract
Pinch Himalayan salt
Seasonal berries to taste

INSTRUCTIONS

1. Take the can of coconut milk out of the refrigerator, open it, scoop out the harden part only with a spoon and transfer into a medium mixing bowl. Discard the water or save for another application.
2. Add maple syrup, vanilla and salt to the mixing bowl.
3. With an electric beater, mix on medium-high until fluffy.
4. Put coconut whipped cream in bowls or tall glasses and add fresh berries.

NOTE

The can of coconut milk needs to be
refrigerated overnight or longer.

FRUIT GUMMIES

YIELD 15 gummies

PREP 5 minutes   TOTAL 5 minutes plus chill time

Ⓝ NUT-FREE

Your family will enjoy these easy-to-make natural fruit gummies made from pure fruit juice, grass-fed gelatin and honey. Grass-fed gelatin has amazing health benefits. It's not only a source of protein but is also absolutely wonderful for the digestive and immune systems as well as for skin, hair, nail, bone and joint health. Choose the best quality juice possible.

INGREDIENTS

1¼ cup 100 percent organic juice, divided (such as blueberry, cherry or mango)
2 tablespoons grass-fed gelatin
¼ cup hot water
2 tablespoons local honey, pure maple syrup or coconut nectar

INSTRUCTIONS

1. In a small mixing bowl, pour ¼ cup juice. Stir in gelatin and whisk until thickened and well-combined.
2. Add hot water to the bowl slowly, whisking constantly so not to create any lumps.
3. Stir in sweetener.
4. Add remaining juice slowly, whisking until well-combined.
5. Pour mixture quickly into a 7x11-inch baking dish.
6. Cover and refrigerate for at least 2 hours or until set.
7. Cut squares with a knife and serve. Keep gummies in the refrigerator.

NOTES

- If you have silicone gummy bear molds or any fun shape molds, use them, especially if making them for children!
- During cold and flu season, try organic orange juice and add 1 ml (30 drops) of echinacea.

HEALTHY JELL-O

SERVES 2-4

PREP 5 minutes   TOTAL 5 minutes plus chill time

Ⓝ NUT-FREE

Jell-O is a dessert enjoyed by many, especially children, but unfortunately, it's not a healthy food. This recipe, however, is healthier as it's made with high-quality ingredients like organic fruit juice, grass-fed gelatin and local honey to sweeten. Gelatin helps to seal the gut lining, promote healthy joints and bones and is a terrific source of amino acids. The Jell-O is delicious served on its own or with coconut whipped cream.

INGREDIENTS

1 ¼ cup organic 100 percent fruit juice, divided
1 tablespoon grass-fed gelatin
½ cup hot water
2 tablespoons local honey or pure maple syrup

INSTRUCTIONS

1. In a small mixing bowl, add ¼ cup of juice. Stir in gelatin and whisk until well-combined.
2. Add hot water slowly to bowl, whisking constantly so as not to create any lumps.
3. Stir in sweetener.
4. Add remaining juice slowly, whisking until well-combined.
5. Pour into a 7x11-inch baking dish.
6. Cover and put in the refrigerator for at least 2 hours or until set.
7. Scoop out with a spoon and serve on its own or with coconut whipped cream.

NOTE

If making the Jell-O with a sour juice like cranberry or pomegranate, you may need to add a little more honey or maple syrup to balance flavors.

COCONUT JASMINE RICE PUDDING

YIELDS 4 cups

PREP 5 minutes   COOK 35 minutes   TOTAL 40 minutes

Ⓝ NUT-FREE

Jasmine rice is an aromatic long grain rice that has a very delicate scent. It's easier to digest and gentler on the digestive tract than brown rice. This recipe combines jasmine rice with coconut milk, maple syrup, cinnamon and vanilla to create a creamy, fragrant and comforting pudding. It can be enjoyed warm or cold and, although lovely for dessert, it can be enjoyed for breakfast too.

INGREDIENTS

1½ cup water

¾ cup jasmine white rice

¼ teaspoon unrefined salt

1 can (13.5 ounces/400 millimeters) full-fat coconut milk

⅓ cup pure maple syrup or mild honey

¾ teaspoon cinnamon

1 tablespoon coconut oil

¾ teaspoon vanilla extract

1 cup unsweetened almond milk or coconut milk

¼ cup raisins or goji berries (optional)

INSTRUCTIONS

1. Rinse rice with cold water and drain.
2. In a medium saucepan, bring water to a boil. Add rice and salt, stir, wait a few seconds until it comes back to a boil, and then turn heat to low. Cover and simmer until rice is cooked and water is all absorbed, about 20 minutes.
3. Stir in coconut milk, maple syrup and cinnamon, and simmer, stirring often, for another 10 minutes to thicken.
4. Remove pot from heat, stir in coconut oil and vanilla, and raisins or goji berries, if using.
5. Allow to cool slightly, stir in almond or coconut milk, and enjoy warm or refrigerate and enjoy cold.

RAW ENERGY BALLS

YIELDS 30-32 balls

PREP 10 minutes   TOTAL 10 minutes plus chill time

These nutrient-dense energy balls are made with dates. They are very nutritious and provide long-lasting energy. They are perfect to bring for outside activities, as they travel well, especially during fall and winter when the weather is cooler.

INGREDIENTS

12 ounces pitted dates (about 2 cups)
1 cup raw almonds
1 cup raw walnuts
1 cup unsweetened coconut flakes
¼ cup goji berries
¼ cup coconut oil, softened or melted
2 tablespoons chia seeds
½ teaspoon ground cinnamon
¼ teaspoon unrefined salt

INSTRUCTIONS

1. Put dates, almonds, walnuts, coconut flakes, goji berries, coconut oil, chia seeds, cinnamon and salt in a food processor and process until well-combined, about 20 to 25 seconds, scraping down sides with a spatula as needed.
2. Form small balls with your hands and place on a cookies sheet.
3. Store in the refrigerator until set.
4. Transfer balls to a container and store in the refrigerator or freezer.

NOTE

The balls will get very soft if left or carried at warm temperatures.

SPICED APPLESAUCE

SERVES 4

PREP 5 minutes   COOK 10 minutes   TOTAL 15 minutes

Ⓝ NUT-FREE

Who doesn't love applesauce? It's hard to resist the smooth texture and the naturally sweet taste of freshly cooked apples, especially when cooked with warming spices like cinnamon and nutmeg. Serve it warm or cold on its own or with yogurt for breakfast, snack or dessert.

INGREDIENTS

6 apples (such as McIntosh, Cortland or Gala),
peeled, cored and chopped

½ cup water

1 tablespoon fresh lemon juice

½ teaspoon ground cinnamon

¼ teaspoon ground nutmeg

⅛ teaspoon ground ginger

Pinch unrefined salt

1 teaspoon vanilla extract

2 tablespoons maple syrup or coconut nectar

INSTRUCTIONS

1. Put apples in a large pot along with water, lemon juice, cinnamon, nutmeg, salt and water.
2. Stir well, bring to a boil, reduce heat to low, cover and simmer until apples are tender, about 6 to 8 minutes.
3. Allow to cool slightly, and then transfer to a blender. Add vanilla and maple syrup and blend until smooth.
4. Serve warm, at room temperature or cold.

NATURAL POPSICLES

These Popsicle recipes are made with natural ingredients and are fun and easy to make. It also makes a great activity to do with children. To unmold easily, run Popsicle mold under room temperature water for a few seconds and twist gently. The number of servings will depend on the size of your Popsicle molds.

ROOIBOS TEA POPSICLES

Rooibos tea (pronounced roo-i-boss) is rich in antioxidants while being caffeine-free and low in tannins. Traditionally, South Africans use rooibos to alleviate infantile colic, allergies, nervous tension, asthma, skin problems and digestive complaints.

INGREDIENTS

¼ cup dried rooibos tea
2 cups hot water
1-2 tablespoons raw or organic honey (optional)

INSTRUCTIONS

1. Infuse rooibos tea leaves in hot water for 10 to 20 minutes.
2. Strain tea and stir in honey if desired.
3. Pour into Popsicle molds and freeze until set.

NOTE

You could also try with lavender or chamomile for a more relaxing treat, especially for babies or toddlers. If serving to babies, omit the sweetener or use maple syrup or coconut nectar – never honey.

COCONUT MANGO POPSICLES

A favorite of many people, this creamy tropical Popsicle is made with coconut milk, mangoes and honey.

INGREDIENTS

1 cup full-fat canned coconut milk
1 cup diced mangoes, fresh or frozen
2 tablespoons organic honey or coconut nectar
¼ teaspoon nonalcoholic vanilla extract
Pinch Himalayan salt

INSTRUCTIONS

1. Put coconut milk, mangoes, honey, vanilla and salt in a blender and blend until smooth.
2. Divide mixture into Popsicle molds and freeze until set.

DAIRY-FREE FUDGE POPSICLES

This very creamy and satisfying fudge recipe will put a smile on both children and adults. Not only its taste is lovely, but it's also a wonderful source of magnesium and antioxidants – thanks to the raw cacao powder.

INGREDIENTS

1 can (14 ounces/400 millimeters)
full-fat coconut milk
¼ cup raw cacao powder
¼ cup pure maple syrup
¼ teaspoon nonalcoholic vanilla extract
Pinch Himalayan salt

INSTRUCTIONS

1. Put coconut milk, cacao powder, maple syrup, vanilla and salt in a blender and blend until smooth.
2. Divide between Popsicle molds and freeze until set.

YUMMY BERRY POPSICLES

I have made this recipe many times – it's that good! It's nutritious, refreshing, naturally sweet and very yummy! If you don't like chunks of fruits in your Popsicles, blend the mixture before dividing it into the molds.

INGREDIENTS

1 cup organic plain whole milk yogurt
1 cup frozen berries (raspberries, blueberries, strawberries or mixed berries)
¼ cup pure maple syrup
¼ teaspoon nonalcoholic vanilla extract
Pinch Himalayan salt

INSTRUCTIONS

1. Put berries in a saucepan and simmer on low heat until softened, about 5 to 6 minutes. Turn off heat, stir in maple syrup, vanilla and salt, and let cool slightly.
2. Gently stir in yogurt, or blend until smooth if you want a smooth texture, and divide between Popsicle molds. Freeze until set.

BAKED GOODS

This section of the book is very unique as it contains healthy yet tasty baked good recipes that are gluten-, dairy- and soy-free and made with natural sweeteners and healthy fats. They are free from refined flours and sugars. Many of them also contain fruits and vegetables. This way, you can bake treats for your family that are healthy, giving you peace of mind. Enjoy!

APPLE CAKE

SERVES 6-9

PREP 20 minutes   COOK 40 minutes   TOTAL 1 hour

NUT-FREE

Made with coconut flour, maple syrup, freshly diced apples and warm-ing spices, this light, moist and flavorful cake is free of refined flour, sugar and vegetable oil. It's an absolutely guilt-free cake perfect for an after-school snack or afternoon tea. It can even be eaten for breakfast.

INGREDIENTS

½ cup coconut flour

¼ cup arrowroot starch

½ teaspoon baking soda

½ teaspoon ground cinnamon

⅛ teaspoon ground nutmeg

⅛ teaspoon ground ginger

⅛ teaspoon unrefined salt

3 pastured eggs

½ cup full-fat canned coconut milk

⅓ cup pure maple syrup

1 teaspoon vanilla extract

4 apples, peeled, cored and diced

Turbinado or coconut sugar, for topping

NOTE

The apples can be diced or sliced. It's a different mouthfeel and look, but it's delicious both ways.

INSTRUCTIONS

1. Preheat oven to 350F.
2. Oil an 8x8-inch cake pan with coconut oil and then line the pan with parchment paper. Set aside.
3. In a large bowl, combine coconut flour, arrowroot, baking soda, cinnamon, nutmeg, ginger and salt. Whisk to combine.
4. In a medium bowl, whisk eggs. Then whisk in coconut milk, maple syrup and vanilla.
5. Pour wet ingredients in with the dry and stir to combine.
6. Fold in apples.
7. Pour batter into the prepared pan.
8. Sprinkle with turbinado or coconut sugar.
9. Bake for 40 minutes or until a toothpick comes out clean.

BANANA BREAD

SERVES 8

PREP 10 minutes   COOK 45 minutes   TOTAL 55 minutes

Ⓝ NUT-FREE

This gluten- and grain-free banana bread made with coconut flour will blow your mind. It's healthy and nutritious while tasting amazing. Enjoy it as a healthy snack, dessert or even for breakfast. It's also fantastic for the lunch box.

INGREDIENTS

⅓ cup coconut flour

⅓ cup arrowroot starch

1 tablespoon ground cinnamon

1 teaspoon baking soda

1 teaspoon baking powder

¼ teaspoon unrefined salt

1½ cup mashed bananas (about 4 ripe bananas)

4 pastured eggs

¼ cup organic honey

¼ cup melted coconut oil

1 teaspoon vanilla extract

1 ripe banana, sliced thinly lengthwise, for topping (optional)

INSTRUCTIONS

1. Preheat oven to 350F.
2. Oil a loaf pan lightly with coconut oil and line with parchment paper. Set aside.
3. Place coconut flour, arrowroot, cinnamon, baking soda, baking powder and salt in a large mixing bowl and whisk to combine.
4. Place mashed banana in a medium mixing bowl. Stir in eggs, honey and vanilla. Add coconut oil and whisk quickly to avoid having the oil solidify and create lumps.
5. Transfer the banana mixture to flour mixture, and stir to combine.
6. Pour batter into the prepared pan.
7. Top with one or two slices of banana if desired.
8. Bake for 45 to 50 minutes or until a toothpick comes out clean.
9. Allow to cool slightly before slicing.

BLUEBERRY LEMON CAKE

PREP 30 minutes   COOK 40 minutes   TOTAL 1 hour, 10 minutes

This gorgeous cake is light and fluffy and loaded with fresh lemon flavor and juicy blueberries. It's a perfect cake to enjoy for afternoon tea, although it's lovely for breakfast too. If you like, drizzle the cake with a honey lemon syrup for additional flavor. .

INGREDIENTS

CAKE

1¼ cup almond flour

¼ cup coconut flour

1 teaspoon baking soda

¼ teaspoon unrefined salt

3 pastured eggs, beaten

¼ cup organic honey

1 lemon, juiced and zested

1 teaspoon vanilla extract

¼ cup melted coconut oil

1 cup blueberries, fresh or frozen

HONEY LEMON SYRUP

2 tablespoons fresh lemon juice

2 tablespoons organic honey

NOTES

- The cake can be stored at room temperature for up to three days or one week in the refrigerator.
- You can substitute honey for maple syrup or coconut nectar.
- If you enjoy lavender, try adding a pinch of culinary lavender to the honey lemon syrup.

INSTRUCTIONS

1. Preheat oven to 350F.
2. Lightly oil a 9-inch round cake pan with coconut oil and line the bottom with parchment paper. Set aside.
3. In a large bowl, combine almond flour, coconut flour, baking soda and salt, and whisk to combine.
4. In a medium bowl, whisk eggs, honey, lemon juice, lemon zest and vanilla, and whisk in coconut oil until combined.
5. Add wet ingredients to dry ingredients and whisk to combine.
6. Add in blueberries and give it a quick stir. Do not overstir as the batter will turn blue and so will your cake.
7. Pour batter into prepared pan.
8. Bake for 35 to 40 minutes or until the edges look golden and a toothpick comes out clean.
9. When the cake is done baking, make the honey lemon syrup if desired. To do so, combine lemon juice and honey in a small saucepan, and heat it gently to melt the honey and allow the glaze to thicken. Turn off heat, allow glaze to cool slightly and drizzle on cake.
10. When cake has cooled, slice and enjoy.

DOUBLE CHOCOLATE ZUCCHINI BREAD

SERVES 8

PREP 20 minutes   COOK 1 hour   TOTAL 1 hour, 20 minutes

Moist, decadent and satisfying, it's hard to believe this chocolate bread is healthy. Made with almond flour, almond butter, eggs, freshly grated zucchini and cacao powder, this loaf makes a nutritious, guilt-free treat for both adults and little ones.

INGREDIENTS

1 cup almond flour

½ cup arrowroot starch

½ cup coconut sugar

⅓ cup raw cacao powder

1 teaspoon baking soda

½ teaspoon unrefined salt

¼ teaspoon ground cinnamon

½ cup organic dark chocolate chips

2 pastured eggs

⅓ cup creamy almond butter

½ cup melted coconut oil

1 teaspoon vanilla extract

2 cups packed shredded zucchini

INSTRUCTIONS

1. Preheat oven to 350F.
2. Oil a loaf pan lightly with coconut oil and line with parchment paper. Set aside.
3. In a large bowl, combine almond flour, arrowroot, coconut sugar, cacao powder, baking soda, salt, cinnamon and chocolate chips. Whisk to combine.
4. In a medium bowl, whisk together eggs, almond butter, melted coconut oil and vanilla extract until well combined. You may also use a small blender for this step.
5. Pour the wet mixture into the dry mixture and mix until combined.
6. Squeeze shredded zucchini with your hands, in batches, to remove as much water as you can. You may also use a colander, cheesecloth or nut milk bag to help remove excess liquid. Add dry zucchini to the bread mixture.
7. Pour batter into the prepared loaf pan.
8. Bake for 1 hour or until a toothpick comes out clean.
9. Allow to cool down before slicing.

OATMEAL RASPBERRY MUFFINS

SERVES 12

PREP 15 minutes   COOK 30 minutes   TOTAL 45 minutes

Ⓝ NUT-FREE

These nutritious oatmeal muffins are crisp from the outside and moist from the inside. They contain ingredients like rolled oats, flaxseeds, cinnamon, coconut oil, banana and berries that are sure to keep you satiated. They are terrific for an on-the-go breakfast or a mid-morning snack and are perfect for the lunch box. For a sweeter muffin, add in mini dark chocolate chips.

INGREDIENTS

2 tablespoons ground flaxseeds

⅓ cup water

1½ cups oat flour

1 cup rolled oats

½ cup coconut sugar

2 teaspoons ground cinnamon

1 teaspoon baking powder

1 teaspoon baking soda

¼ teaspoon unrefined salt

2 small ripe bananas (about ¾ cup mashed)

¼ cup pure maple syrup or honey

¼ cup melted coconut oil

1 teaspoon vanilla extract

½ cup unsweetened almond or coconut milk

1 cup frozen raspberries

½ cup mini vegan or dark chocolate chips (optional)

INSTRUCTIONS

1. Preheat oven to 350F.
2. In a small bowl, combine ground flaxseeds with water, stir and set aside.
3. Line a 12-cup muffin tin with liners. Set aside.
4. Combine oat flour, rolled oats, coconut sugar, cinnamon, baking powder, baking soda and salt in a large mixing bowl and whisk to combine.
5. Mash banana in a medium mixing bowl with maple syrup, coconut oil and vanilla. Stir to combine. Add in flaxseed mixture, stir, and add in almond milk slowly.
6. Pour wet ingredients into dry and stir until well combined.
7. Add in raspberries and chocolate chips if using and stir again.
8. Divide batter between muffin tins, filling each cup completely.
9. Bake for 30 minutes or until a toothpick comes out clean.

NOTES

- Muffins will last about 4 days at room temperature or up to 1 week in the refrigerator. They can be frozen as well.
- You can make oat flour at home by putting rolled oats into a food processor and processing until very smooth. Keep the flour in a labeled glass jar in the refrigerator.
- If you prefer, use another flour like spelt, six grains or whole wheat. However, they won't be gluten-free.
- You can also use frozen blueberries or a berry mixture.

MORNING GLORY MUFFINS

MAKES 12 muffins

PREP 15 minutes   COOK 20 minutes   TOTAL 35 minutes

Ⓝ NUT-FREE

Crisp on the outside and moist on the inside, these vegan, flourless morning glory muffins make an excellent breakfast or morning snack. They are wonderful for breakfast on-the-go or for the lunch box. It's also a pleasant way to help your child eat more fruits and vegetables.

INGREDIENTS

2 tablespoons ground flaxseeds

¼ cup water

2½ cups gluten-free rolled oats

½ cup chopped walnuts and/or sunflower seeds

½ cup unsweetened coconut flakes

¼ cup raisins

1 teaspoon ground cinnamon

1 teaspoon baking powder

½ teaspoon baking soda

½ teaspoon unrefined salt

1 cup shredded zucchini, from about 1 medium zucchini

1 cup shredded carrots, from about 2 medium carrots

1 apple, shredded

¼ cup melted coconut oil

¼ cup organic honey or pure maple syrup

INSTRUCTIONS

1. Preheat oven to 350F and line a muffin tin with muffin paper. Set aside.
2. Combine ground flaxseeds with ¼ cup water in a small bowl. Stir well and set aside.
3. Put rolled oats into a food processor and pulse a few times to break down the oats.
4. Put oats into a large mixing bowl along with the walnuts, coconut flakes, raisins, cinnamon, baking powder, baking soda and salt, and give it a stir.
5. Combine shredded zucchini, carrots and apple with coconut oil, honey and flax mixture in a medium mixing bowl. Stir well, and pour into the dry mixture and stir again to combine.
6. Divide batter into muffin tins and bake for 20 minutes or until the edges look golden and crisp.
7. Store muffins in an airtight container for up to 3 days or refrigerate them for up to a week. They also freeze very well.

SUGAR-FREE OAT COOKIES

YIELDS 14 cookies

PREP 10 minutes   COOK 12 minutes   TOTAL 22 minutes

Ⓘ NUT-FREE

These thick and chewy oatmeal cookies are very nutritious and free from added sugars. They are sweetened with banana and dates – two naturally sweet and mineral-rich fruits. These cookies are wonderful for the lunch box, as a healthy snack or to bring during outside activities.

INGREDIENTS

1 cup oat flour
¾ cup quick cooking oats
1 ½ teaspoon baking powder
1 ½ teaspoon ground cinnamon
Pinch unrefined salt
½ cup mashed banana

½ cup puréed dates, homemade or store-bought
¼ cup coconut oil
1 pastured egg
1 teaspoon vanilla extract
½ cup raisins, chocolate chips or chopped walnuts (optional)

INSTRUCTIONS

1. Preheat oven to 350F.
2. Line a large baking sheet with parchment paper. Set aside.
3. Combine oat flour, quick cooking oats, cinnamon and salt in a mixing bowl and stir to combine.
4. In a separate bowl, combine mashed banana, dates, coconut oil, egg and vanilla, and whisk to combine.
5. Add wet ingredients to dry and whisk again. If using raisins, chocolate chips or walnuts, add them and stir to combine.
6. Scoop out about 2 tablespoons of the dough, place on baking sheet and flatten up gently with your fingers. Repeat with the remaining dough.
7. Bake for 12 minutes.

NOTE

To make date purée at home, remove pits from 1 cup of dates, soak them in water for at least 30 minutes to soften them up, then add them to your food processor and run until smooth, scraping down sides as needed.

PEANUT BUTTER COOKIES

SERVES 18

PREP 15 minutes   COOK 15 minutes   TOTAL 30 minutes

Hello, peanut butter cookie lovers! I hope you enjoy this healthier recipe made with natural peanut butter, coconut sugar and flaxseeds. They are moist, rich and very peanut buttery. My family loves them. It's one of those recipes for cookies that never stay long in the cookie jar when I make them.

INGREDIENTS

1 tablespoon ground flaxseeds or chia seeds

3 tablespoons water

1 cup creamy peanut butter, preferably organic or homemade

¾ cup coconut sugar

½ teaspoon vanilla extract

¼ teaspoon unrefined salt

INSTRUCTIONS

1. Preheat oven to 350F.
2. Line a large baking sheet with parchment paper. Set aside.
3. In a small bowl, mix ground flaxseeds or chia seeds with water, stir, and set aside.
4. In a large bowl, add peanut butter, coconut sugar, vanilla and salt. Whisk to combine.
5. When the seeds have absorbed all the water, add to the bowl with the peanut butter mix and whisk again until combined well.
6. Take about a tablespoon of the batter, form a ball with your hands and place on the cookie sheet. Repeat with the remaining dough.
7. Using a fork, lightly press each cookie to form both vertical and horizontal lines. Dip the tablespoon scoop in hot water between each cookie to prevent sticking. Cookies won't spread, so they can be close to each other.
8. Bake for 15 minutes or until the edges look golden.

NOTES

If there is a peanut allergy in your family or you are avoiding legumes, use creamy almond butter.

PUMPKIN SQUARES

SERVES 16

PREP 5 minutes   COOK 20 minutes   TOTAL 25 minutes

Ⓝ NUT-FREE

These light, moist and fluffy pumpkin squares are flavored with seasonal spices for a healthy autumn treat. Use homemade or canned pumpkin purée. They are best eaten the same day.

INGREDIENTS

¾ cup pumpkin purée, homemade or canned

½ cup creamy almond butter

¼ cup pure maple syrup

2 pastured eggs

2 teaspoons ground cinnamon

¼ teaspoon ground nutmeg

1 teaspoon vanilla extract

½ teaspoon baking soda

¼ teaspoon unrefined salt

Unsweetened coconut flakes, to sprinkle on top (optional)

INSTRUCTIONS

1. Preheat oven to 350F.
2. Line an 8x8-inch baking dish with parchment paper. Set aside.
3. In a blender, combine pumpkin purée, almond butter, maple syrup, eggs, cinnamon, nutmeg, vanilla, baking soda and salt, and blend until smooth.
4. Pour the mixture into the prepared pan and shake the pan gently to distribute the batter evenly.
5. Sprinkle with coconut flakes if desired.
6. Bake until the color is slightly golden on top and a toothpick comes out clean, about 18 to 20 minutes.
7. Allow to cool before cutting into squares.

NOTE

For a nut-free alternative, replace the almond butter with tahini.

SUGAR COOKIES

YIELDS 16 cookies

PREP 10 minutes   COOK 15 minutes   TOTAL 25 minutes

You won't believe how delicious these healthy sugar cookies are. My family enjoys them, especially when I make them during the holidays. They are very easy to make – no mixer needed – and cookie cutters can be used to make fun shapes. These cookies are sure to disappear quickly.

INGREDIENTS

1 cup almond flour

½ cup arrowroot starch

¼ teaspoon baking soda

¼ teaspoon unrefined salt

¼ cup melted coconut oil

¼ cup pure maple syrup

1 teaspoon vanilla extract

Organic powdered sugar or coconut butter frosting (optional)

COCONUT BUTTER FROSTING

½ cup coconut butter

2 tablespoons pure maple syrup

½ teaspoon vanilla extract

Pinch Himalayan salt

2 tablespoons almond milk

NOTES

- The dough can be made in advance and stored in the refrigerator.
- Watch the cookies carefully as they could be done quicker than listed if your oven runs hot.
- The cookies can be frozen.

INSTRUCTIONS

1. Preheat oven to 325F.
2. Line a large baking sheet with parchment paper. Set aside.
3. Combine almond flour, arrowroot starch, baking soda and salt in a large bowl and whisk to combine.
4. In a separate bowl, whisk coconut oil, maple syrup and vanilla quickly.
5. Transfer liquid to dry ingredients and whisk to combine.
6. Scoop 1 tablespoon of dough and form a ball with your hands. Place on the cookie sheet and press with your fingers gently to form cookies. Repeat with remaining dough.
7. Bake until the edges look slightly crisp and golden, about 12 to 15 minutes.
8. Once cooled, frost cookies or sprinkle them with powdered sugar if desired.
9. To make the coconut butter frosting, put coconut butter, maple syrup, vanilla and salt in a food processor and process until smooth, scraping sides down as needed. Add almond milk slowly, 1 tablespoon at a time. Frost cookies after they have cooled completely.

FLOURLESS BROWNIES

PREP 10 minutes   COOK 20 minutes   TOTAL 30 minutes

These moist, rich and decadent double chocolate brownies are flourless and made with ingredients like almond butter, avocado and coconut oil. You won't believe how delicious they are when you taste them!

INGREDIENTS

½ cup creamy almond butter

½ cup mashed avocado (about 1 medium)

2 pastured eggs

⅓ cup local honey or pure maple syrup

⅓ cup coconut oil

¼ cup organic cacao powder

1 teaspoon vanilla extract

½ teaspoon baking soda

¼ teaspoon unrefined salt

¾ cup dark chocolate chips or 70% (or more) dark chocolate, finely chopped

INSTRUCTIONS

1. Preheat oven to 350F.
2. Oil an 8x8-inch baking dish lightly and line with parchment paper. Set aside.
3. In a blender or food processor, add almond butter, avocado, eggs, honey, coconut oil, cacao powder, vanilla, baking soda and salt, and blend until smooth.
4. Add chocolate chips and stir with a spoon.
5. Pour batter into prepared pan and spread evenly with a silicone or offset spatula.
6. Bake for 25 to 30 minutes or until a toothpick comes out clean.
7. Allow to cool before slicing into squares.
8. Store the brownies in an airtight container. They can also be frozen.

NOTES

If there is a nut allergy to consider, use tahini or sunflower seed butter instead of almond butter.

BLACKSTRAP MOLASSES COOKIES

YIELDS 20 cookies

PREP 15 minutes   COOK 12 minutes   TOTAL 27 minutes

Crisp on the outside and moist from the inside, these blackstrap mo-lasses cookies are sweet and slightly spicy and make a perfect winter or holiday treat.

INGREDIENTS

1½ cup almond flour

½ cup arrowroot flour

¼ cup coconut sugar, plus more
    to garnish if desired

½ teaspoon baking soda

¾ teaspoon ground ginger

½ teaspoon ground cinnamon

⅛ teaspoon ground cloves

⅛ teaspoon unrefined salt

1 pastured egg

1 teaspoon vanilla extract

2 tablespoons blackstrap molasses

2 tablespoons softened or melted coconut oil

NOTE

Using cookie cutters to make shapes is possible, although not as easy as with other cookie doughs. To do so, make sure the dough is always cold. Roll the dough between two sheets of parchment paper to avoid sticking and help get a uniform thickness. Cut with your favorite shaped cutters.

INSTRUCTIONS

1. Preheat oven to 325F.
2. Line a large baking sheet with parchment paper. Set aside.
3. Combine almond flour, arrowroot flour, coconut sugar, baking soda, ground ginger, cinnamon, cloves and salt in a large mixing bowl, and whisk to combine.
4. In a separate bowl, whisk together the egg with the vanilla and molasses, and whisk coconut oil in quickly.
5. Transfer wet ingredients to dry ingredients and whisk until combined well.
6. Scoop out about 1 tablespoon of the dough and roll in your hands to form a ball. Place on cookie sheet and repeat with all the dough.
7. Press on each ball gently to flatten cookies, using either your hands or a fork that is dipped in warm water after each pressing to avoid sticking.
8. Sprinkle cookies with coconut sugar if desired.
9. Bake for 12 minutes or until edges look slightly crisp.

VANILLA BIRTHDAY CAKE

YIELDS 2 layers of cake

SERVES 8

PREP 20 minutes   COOK 30 minutes   TOTAL 50 minutes

This birthday cake was created for my son's first birthday. I wanted a moist, flavorful and healthy cake without any refined flour, sugar, oil, artificial flavors or artificial colors. The result is a cake made with almond flour, pastured eggs, coconut oil and maple syrup that is surprisingly easy to make. It can be made for any occasion or even just as a healthy snack. It's tasty even without the frosting.

INGREDIENTS

CAKE
1½ cups almond flour
2 tablespoons arrowroot powder
1 teaspoon baking powder
¼ teaspoon unrefined salt
2 pastured eggs
½ cup unsweetened almond or coconut milk
¼ cup pure maple syrup
2 tablespoons melted coconut oil
2 teaspoons vanilla extract

FROSTING
1 can (13.5 ounces/400 milliliters) full-fat coconut milk, refrigerated overnight
1 tablespoon pure maple syrup
½ teaspoon vanilla extract
Pinch unrefined salt

OPTIONAL TOPPINGS
Berries
Seasonal fruits
Coconut flakes
Dark chocolate curls

1. Preheat oven to 350F.
2. If your jar of coconut oil is solidified, place in a bowl with hot water for a few minutes or until ready to use.
3. Oil two round 6-inch cake pans lightly with coconut oil and line the bottom with parchment paper. Set aside.
4. In a large mixing bowl, sift almond flour with arrowroot powder, baking powder, salt and cacao powder if using.
5. In a medium mixing bowl, whisk the eggs with almond milk, pure maple syrup, melted coconut oil and vanilla until well-combined.
6. Pour wet ingredients into dry and whisk to combine.
7. Divide batter evenly between pans.
8. Bake for about 30 minutes or until a toothpick comes out clean.
9. Allow to cool completely before spreading frosting.
10. To make frosting, open the can of refrigerated coconut milk and scoop out the hardest part only, discarding the liquid or keeping it to use for smoothies. Place the coconut 'cream' in a mixing bowl, and add maple syrup, vanilla and salt. Using an electric mixer, beat until smooth and there are no more lumps. Refrigerate frosting until ready to use.
11. Frost cake once cooled, adding any additional topping if desired, and refrigerate cake until ready to serve.

NOTES

- For a 4-layer cake, double the recipe.
- For a chocolate cake, add ¼ cup of cacao powder to the batter.
- Do not use light coconut milk, and do not shake the can, otherwise, it won't whip.
- Make sure you cannot hear the liquid when you shake your can of refrigerated coconut milk. If you can hear the liquid, it means the cream of the coconut milk is already mixed with the water, and you won't be able to scoop out the hard cream.
- For a colorful frosting, use natural food coloring or make your own using fruits, vegetables or spice powders.

VANILLA CUPCAKES WITH CHOCOLATE FROSTING

YIELDS 12 cupcakes

PREP 15 minutes   COOK 20 minutes   TOTAL 35 minutes

NUT-FREE

These healthy cupcakes are delightful. They are light, moist and nutritious. They are free from grains, gluten, nuts, dairy products and refined sugars. The chocolate frosting is made with avocados, cacao powder and coconut oil and is light, creamy and fluffy. You can also use your favorite healthy frosting recipe if you prefer.

INGREDIENTS

¾ cup coconut flour
½ teaspoon baking powder
½ teaspoon baking soda
¼ teaspoon unrefined salt
6 pastured eggs
½ cup pure maple syrup or organic honey

⅓ cup melted coconut oil
¼ cup almond or coconut milk
1 tablespoon vanilla extract

Chocolate avocado frosting (page 313)
   or favorite healthy frosting

INSTRUCTIONS

1. Preheat oven to 350F.
2. Line a 12-cup muffin tin with liners and set aside.
3. In a large mixing bowl, mix coconut flour, baking powder, baking soda and salt.
4. In a medium bowl, beat eggs and whisk in maple syrup, coconut oil, almond milk and vanilla.
5. Add wet ingredients to dry ingredients and mix to combine.
6. Divide batter evenly between the 12 muffin cups.
7. Bake for 20 minutes or until the edges look slightly golden and a toothpick comes out clean.
8. Make frosting and frost cupcakes once cooled.
9. Store cupcakes in the refrigerator until ready to serve.

MILK, SAUCES AND MORE

In the next few pages, you will find sweet recipes like nut milk, chia jam, chocolate hazelnut spread, and superfood hot chocolate to more savory recipes like almond bread-crumbs, tahini sauce and cashew sour cream. They are all gluten-, grain- and dairy-free.

For the moms, I also created a healthy Frappuccino recipe to help you get through the day. I thought you might enjoy a special treat created just for you!

ALMOND MILK

YIELD 4 cups

PREP 10 minutes   TOTAL 10 minutes

Almond milk is easy to make and so incredibly delicious. It's no comparison to store-bought almond milk. Not only do you control the ratio of almonds to water and make the nutrients easier to digest by soaking almonds overnight, but you also have a nut milk that is free from added refined sugar, synthetic vitamins, additives or preservatives. All you will need is a blender and a nut milk bag or cheesecloth.

INGREDIENTS

1 cup raw almonds
4 cups filtered water
Pinch Himalayan salt
1 teaspoon vanilla extract (optional)
1-2 Medjool dates, pitted (optional)

NOTES

- If you drink a lot of almond milk, try making the recipe with 5 cups of water so that it lasts a little longer.
- You can purchase a nut milk bag at your health food store or online. It's reusable so, once you are done with it, rinse it well, let it dry and put it away until next time.
- Store the almond pulp in the refrigerator and use it to add to smoothies or baked goods, to make raw crackers or cookies or almond flour or breadcrumbs. You can even use it to make face scrubs!

INSTRUCTIONS

1. Place almonds in a bowl and cover with water. Let almonds soak overnight.
2. In the morning, drain almonds in a colander to discard soaking water. Rinse well and place almonds in a blender.
3. Add 4 cups of filtered water and salt as well as vanilla and Medjool dates if using, and blend until smooth.
4. Strain in a nut milk bag or cheesecloth over a large bowl. Squeeze with your hands slowly to extract the milk. You will need to squeeze harder toward the end to get as much milk out as possible. Almond pulp should be relatively dry.
5. Store the milk into a large glass container in the refrigerator for up to 4 days.
6. Shake before using.

QUICK ALMOND MILK

SERVES 4-6

PREP 10 minutes   TOTAL 10 minutes

If you are short on time or don't have a nut milk bag or cheesecloth, try this quick recipe using almond butter. Get a good quality almond butter, preferably raw or homemade, or make sure there are only almonds listed on the ingredient list.

INGREDIENTS

¼ cup almond butter
1 cup filtered water
½ teaspoon vanilla extract (optional)
1 Medjool date (optional)
Pinch Himalayan salt (optional)

INSTRUCTIONS

1. In a blender, put almond butter and water, and vanilla, date and salt if using, and blend until smooth.
2. Store the milk in a large glass container in the refrigerator for up to 4 days.
3. Shake before using.

HEMP SEED MILK

YIELD 4 cups

PREP 5 minutes   TOTAL 5 minutes

Ⓢ NUT-FREE

Hemp seed milk is the easiest and most nutritious milk to make. There is no straining needed, meaning the whole seed is used. Hemp seeds are extremely nutritious. They are rich in protein, fiber, healthy fats and various minerals. Use it the same way you would use other milks.

INGREDIENTS

½ cup shelled hemp seeds
4 cups filtered water
Pinch Himalayan salt
¼ teaspoon pure vanilla extract (optional)
1-2 Medjool dates, pitted (optional)

INSTRUCTIONS

1. In a high-speed blender, place hemp seeds, water and salt as well as vanilla and dates if using, and blend until smooth.
2. Store milk in a glass container in the refrigerator for up to 4 days.
3. Shake before using.

STRAWBERRY MILK

YIELD 2 cups

PREP 5 minutes   TOTAL 5 minutes

This slightly sweet milk made with fresh almond milk and strawberries is a nutritious treat for children. Make sure the strawberries are fresh and, preferably organic or local for better taste and sweetness.

INGREDIENTS

2 cups almond milk, homemade
or unsweetened
1 cup fresh strawberries
1 Medjool date or 1 tablespoon honey,
maple syrup or coconut nectar
¼ teaspoon pure vanilla extract

INSTRUCTIONS

1. Combine all ingredients in a blender. Blend until nice and smooth.
2. Store in a glass container in the refrigerator up to four days.
3. Shake before using.

NOTE

You can make creamy ice pops with this recipe by filling ice pop molds with the milk!

CHOCOLATE MILK

YIELD 2 cups

PREP 5 minutes   TOTAL 5 minutes

🥜 NUT-FREE

Your children will enjoy this healthy chocolate milk. It tastes surprisingly similar to traditional chocolate milk, although less sweet. For extra sweetness, use an extra date or two.

INGREDIENTS

2 cups almond, coconut or hemp
milk, preferably homemade
2-3 Medjool dates, pitted
2 tablespoons raw cacao powder

INSTRUCTIONS

1. Put almond milk, dates and cacao powder in a blender and blend until smooth.
2. Transfer to a glass container and store it in the refrigerator for up to 4 days.
3. Shake before using.

COCONUT MILK

YIELD 4 cups

PREP 5 minutes   TOTAL 5 minutes

Ⓘ NUT-FREE

There are a few different ways to prepare coconut milk. My absolute favorite is by using young Thai coconuts. But, as they are not available everywhere, this recipe uses coconut flakes instead for convenience. The taste and texture are lovely, and the milk is relatively easy to make, although it needs to be strained.

INGREDIENTS

1 cups unsweetened raw coconut flakes
4 cups filtered water
Pinch Himalayan salt

1 teaspoon vanilla extract (optional)
2 Medjool dates, pitted (optional)

INSTRUCTIONS

1. In a high-speed blender, combine coconut flakes, filtered water and salt as well as vanilla and dates if using. Blend on medium-high speed for 1 to 2 minutes or until you get a uniform mixture.
2. Over a large bowl, pour the coconut milk through a nut milk bag or cheesecloth slowly and squeeze the milk out gently. Use more pressure toward the end to get as much milk out as possible. The pulp should be dry.
3. Store milk in a glass container in the refrigerator for up to 4 days.
4. Shake before using.

NOTES

- Coconut pulp can be kept and stored in the refrigerator to add to different recipes like granola, smoothies or baked goods.
- Although coconut is not a nut, it is an allergen for some people.

MOM'S FRAPPUCCINO

SERVES 1

PREP 5 minutes   TOTAL 5 minutes

Ⓝ NUT-FREE

Moms, this recipe is all for you – not meant to share! Enjoy it as an afternoon pick-me-up or even as a breakfast smoothie. It will help you go through the day but in a healthy way. If you'd like an even creamier and more nutritious Frappuccino, add some almond butter and an herbal adaptogen like maca to support energy levels and balance hormones.

INGREDIENTS

1 cup unsweetened vanilla almond or coconut milk
1 shot espresso or 1 teaspoon instant coffee
2 Medjool dates, pitted
1 tablespoon raw cacao powder
1 tablespoon local organic honey or pure maple syrup
Pinch ground cinnamon
Pinch Himalayan salt
2 cups ice cubes
1 tablespoon almond butter (optional)
1 teaspoon maca (optional)

INSTRUCTIONS

1. In a high-speed blender, add milk, espresso or coffee, dates, cacao powder, honey, cinnamon and salt, along with almond butter and maca if using. Add ice cubes and blend until smooth. Enjoy immediately if possible.

BEDTIME MOLASSES DRINK

SERVES 1

PREP 5 minutes   TOTAL 5 minutes

This nourishing bedtime drink is made with milk, blackstrap molasses, cinnamon, nutmeg and Himalayan salt. Milk and molasses are known to support sleep as they are a rich source of calcium and magnesium. Calcium is necessary for the brain to convert tryptophan into melatonin, a sleep-inducing substance, and magnesium increases gamma-Aminobutyric acid (GABA), which encourages relaxation and sleep. Cinnamon helps regulate blood sugar, nutmeg is considered to be a strong sedative and Himalayan salt is rich in minerals that improve sleep. It's a delicious and satisfying beverage that is best to be consumed 30 minutes to 1 hour before bedtime.

INGREDIENTS

1 cup organic whole milk, goat milk or unsweetened almond milk
1 tablespoon blackstrap molasses
⅛ teaspoon Himalayan salt
⅛ teaspoon ground cinnamon
Pinch ground nutmeg

INSTRUCTIONS

1. Blend the milk, molasses, salt and cinnamon if using until smooth.
2. Heat in a saucepan until warm.
3. Pour into a glass and enjoy immediately.

NOTE

If dairy-free, almond milk is a good alternative to cow's milk or goat's milk as it also contains both calcium and tryptophan. Homemade almond milk is best. Otherwise, use unsweetened.

NATURAL ELECTROLYTE DRINK

SERVES 4

PREP 5 minutes   5 minutes

Ⓝ NUT-FREE

Whether it's to consume on a hot summer day or to fill your child's bottle during a sporting event, this healthy drink will replenish and rehydrate the body naturally. There are no artificial sweeteners, flavors, colors or preservatives in this beverage – only real, natural ingredients. Coconut water, which contains five electrolytes (sodium, potassium, calcium, magnesium and phosphorus) as well as vitamin C and natural carbohydrates is combined with fresh lemon juice, organic honey and unrefined salt for more nutrition, energy, electrolytes and flavors.

INGREDIENTS

2 cups coconut water, preferably raw
2 cups cold water
1 lemon, juiced
1 tablespoon organic or local honey
⅛ teaspoon Himalayan salt

INSTRUCTIONS

1. Put coconut water, water, lemon juice, honey and salt in a blender and blend until smooth.
2. Transfer to a glass bottle and store in the refrigerator.
3. Drink cold.

NOTE

When buying coconut water, look for brands with a minimal ingredient list or that contains raw coconut water. If you have access to young Thai coconuts where you live, get a few and cut at home when needed.

SUPERFOOD HOT CHOCOLATE

SERVES 2-4

PREP 2 minutes   COOK 3 minutes   TOTAL 5 minutes

Ⓝ NUT-FREE

Stay warm and cozy this winter while boosting your immune system with this hot chocolate. Made with superfoods like raw cacao powder, coconut oil and cinnamon, this hot cacao beverage is rich in vitamins, minerals, antioxidants and healthy fats. If you like, add a scoop of collagen to benefit from its immune-, digestive- and beauty-boosting properties, and top with a dollop of coconut whipped cream for extra fun and yumminess!

INGREDIENTS

1½ cups unsweetened almond milk

2 tablespoons raw cacao powder

2 tablespoons coconut sugar

1 tablespoon almond butter

1 teaspoon coconut oil

Pinch ground cinnamon

Pinch unrefined salt

1 scoop bovine- or marine-sourced collagen peptides (optional)

Coconut whipped cream, to garnish (optional)

INSTRUCTIONS

1. Put almond milk in a small saucepan and heat it on low heat until warm.
2. Transfer almond milk to a blender and add cacao powder, coconut sugar, almond butter, coconut oil, cinnamon and salt and collagen if using.
3. Blend until smooth and frothy.
4. Pour into a mug or two and garnish with coconut whipped cream if desired.

NOTES

- If you want a caffeine-free hot chocolate, try with carob powder instead of cacao.
- For a nut-free alternative, skip the almond butter.

HOMEMADE ALMOND BUTTER

YIELD 1½ cup

PREP 5 to 20 minutes   COOK 15 minutes   TOTAL 20 to 35 minutes

Creamy homemade almond butter made with almonds only – no added oil or salt. It's absolutely divine. Use raw or roasted almonds, depending on your personal taste, or get raw almonds and roast them yourself to improve flavors and decrease time in the food processor

INGREDIENTS

3 cups raw or roasted almonds

INSTRUCTIONS

1. Optional step: Preheat oven to 350F. Place raw almonds on a baking sheet and roast in preheated oven for about 12 to 15 minutes. Allow to cool slightly and add to a food processor.
2. Place almonds in a large food processor and process until creamy, about 20 minutes, stopping occasionally to scrape down the sides with a silicone spatula. If you have roasted the almonds first, they will turn into almond butter very rapidly, about 2 minutes.
3. Store in a glass jar and keep in the refrigerator. It will keep for a few weeks.

ALMOND 'BREADCRUMBS'

YIELD 1 cup

PREP 5 minutes   COOK 2 minutes   TOTAL 7 minutes

Whether it's to coat a piece of fish or chicken, add into meatballs or sprinkle on top of casseroles or side dishes, this bread-free breadcrumbs recipe is healthy, crunchy and so very flavorful!

INGREDIENTS

1 cup raw almonds
½ teaspoon garlic powder
¼ teaspoon unrefined salt
2 tablespoons extra-virgin olive oil
¼ teaspoon Italian seasoning (optional)

INSTRUCTIONS

1. Add almonds, garlic powder, salt and Italian seasonings, if using, to a food processor. Process until mostly smooth but leaving some chunks for texture, about 10 seconds.
2. Heat oil in a skillet over medium heat. Add almond mixture and cook until it starts to get fragrant and golden in color, about 2 minutes.
3. Allow to cool and use immediately or store in an airtight container in the refrigerator for up to 2 weeks.

NOTE

Although these breadcrumbs taste better after being toasted in oil in the skillet, they can be used right from the food processor for a quick or raw alternative.

CASHEW AIOLI

YIELD 1 cup

PREP 5 minutes   TOTAL 5 minutes

Creamy, flavorful sauce made out of cashews, perfect to serve with fish cakes or vegetarian patties, as a spread for sandwiches or burgers or as a dip for vegetables.

INGREDIENTS

1 cup raw cashews
¾ cup filtered water
¼ cup fresh lemon juice
1 clove garlic, finely chopped
½ teaspoon Dijon mustard
¾ teaspoon unrefined salt

INSTRUCTIONS

1. Place cashews in a bowl and fill with water. Place on counter and let soak for 1 to 4 hours. Drain in a colander, rinse under running water and add cashews to a blender.
2. Add in filtered water, lemon juice, garlic, Dijon and salt, and blend until smooth, scraping down the sides as needed with a silicone spatula.
3. Transfer to a bowl and enjoy immediately or store in the refrigerator.

CASHEW 'SOUR CREAM'

YIELD 1 cup

PREP 5 minutes   TOTAL 5 minutes

Creamy 'sour cream' made with raw cashews perfect for food like loaded sweet potatoes, nachos or enchiladas. Make sure to soak the nuts in water prior using them as it makes blending easier and makes nutrients easier to absorb in the body.

INGREDIENTS

1 cup raw cashews
½ cup filtered water
1 lemon, juiced
½ teaspoon unrefined salt

INSTRUCTIONS

1. Place cashews in a bowl and fill with water. Place on counter and let soak for 1 to 4 hours. Drain in a colander, rinse under running water and add cashews to blender.
2. Add in filtered water, lemon juice and salt. Blend until smooth. Add 1 to 2 tablespoon more water if needed.
3. Transfer to a bowl and enjoy immediately or store in the refrigerator.

NOTE

If serving later, you may need to add a little more water as it will thicken in the refrigerator.

CHOCOLATE AVOCADO FROSTING

YIELD 1½ cup

PREP 10 minutes   TOTAL 10 minutes

This light, fluffy and creamy chocolate avocado frosting is perfect to add on top of cakes, cupcakes or even brownies. It's free from powdered sugar, shortening and butter. Instead, features ingredients like avocados, raw cacao powder, maple syrup and coconut oil. The frosting tastes so good that you will want to eat it by the spoonful!

INGREDIENTS

2 ripe avocados
½ cup raw cacao powder
½ cup pure maple syrup or local honey
2 tablespoons coconut oil
½ teaspoon vanilla extract
⅛ teaspoon Himalayan salt

INSTRUCTIONS

1. Place the flesh of the avocados into a food processor. Add raw cacao powder, maple syrup, coconut oil, vanilla and salt, and process until smooth, scraping down sides as needed.
2. Use frosting immediately or store in the refrigerator until ready to use. It's best to use within the same day.

CHOCOLATE HAZELNUT SPREAD

YIELD 2 cups

PREP 25 minutes   COOK 20 minutes   TOTAL 45 minutes

This creamy, chocolaty vegan hazelnut spread tastes heavenly. It's made with freshly roasted hazelnuts, dark chocolate, coconut oil and pure maple syrup – no refined sugar, modified vegetable oil or skim milk powder in there. Your family will love and enjoy this nutritious, guilt-free treat!

INGREDIENTS

2 cups raw hazelnuts

1 (3.5-ounce/100-gram) dark chocolate bar, cut into chunks

2 tablespoons coconut oil

⅓ cup pure maple syrup

½ cup unsweetened coconut or almond milk

⅛ teaspoon Himalayan salt

INSTRUCTIONS

1. Preheat oven to 350F.
2. Spread the hazelnuts in a single layer on a baking sheet and toast them until they are browned and fragrant, about 12 to 15 minutes.
3. Put hazelnuts between kitchen or paper towels and rub with your hands to remove any loose skins. Discard skins and put hazelnuts into a food processor.
4. Start to blend at low speed and increase slowly until nuts turn to butter, about 2 minutes. Add chocolate to a bain-marie or saucepan and let it melt completely over low heat.
5. Add coconut oil to chocolate and use a silicone spatula to combine.
6. Add chocolate mixture to hazelnut butter and blend until smooth.
7. Add in maple syrup, coconut milk and salt, and blend again until smooth.
8. Pour into a glass jar and store at room temperature for a few weeks.

RASPBERRY CHIA JAM

YIELD 1 cup

PREP 5 minutes   COOK 15 minutes   TOTAL 20 minutes

Ⓝ NUT-FREE

Making homemade jam has never been easier! In less than 20 minutes, you will have a tasty and nutritious jam made with chia seeds to use like usual on toast or to top yogurt, smoothie bowls, oatmeal, pancakes, waffles or cakes!

INGREDIENTS

2 cups raspberries, fresh or frozen
2 tablespoons chia seeds
3 tablespoons organic honey, maple syrup or coconut nectar
1 teaspoon fresh lemon juice
Pinch Himalayan salt

INSTRUCTIONS

1. In a medium saucepan over low heat, add raspberries, cover and simmer, stirring often, until raspberries have softened, about 10 to 12 minutes.
2. Add chia seeds, honey, lemon juice and salt. Stir to combine and break down larger pieces of raspberries with a wooden spoon.
3. Let sit for 10 to 15 minutes and transfer to an airtight container.
4. Transfer jam to a glass jar and store in the refrigerator for up to 2 weeks.

NOTE

You can try the recipe with any other berries.
Keep in mind, however, that the flavor will change.

EASY HOMEMADE KETCHUP

YIELD 1¾ cup

PREP 5 minutes   TOTAL 5 minutes

🥜 NUT-FREE

Have you ever thought about making your own ketchup? If not, you may want to give this a try. It's healthier than the store-bought versions; you know exactly what's in it and it's quick and easy to make. All you need are a few ingredients, a whisk and bowl.

INGREDIENTS

2 cans (6 ounces/170 grams) tomato paste
¼ cup apple cider vinegar
¼ cup pure maple syrup
1 tablespoon onion powder
1 teaspoon garlic powder
1 teaspoon unrefined salt
¼ teaspoon ground black pepper
⅓ cup filtered water

INSTRUCTIONS

1. Put tomato paste, apple cider vinegar, maple syrup, onion powder, garlic powder, salt, black pepper and water in a mixing bowl and whisk until well combined. Add a little more water if you prefer thinner ketchup.
2. Transfer in a glass container with a good seal and store in the refrigerator. It will last for a few weeks if stored properly.

NOTE

For an extra kick, add a pinch of cayenne pepper.

SMOOTH TOMATO SAUCE

YIELD 8 cups

PREP 5 minutes   COOK 40 minutes   TOTAL 45 minutes

Ⓝ NUT-FREE

This easy-to-make tomato sauce is smooth and flavorful. It works beautifully with the turkey meatballs recipe but can be used in any pasta dishes or Italian recipes that require a tomato sauce. For the best flavor, use San Marzano tomatoes.

INGREDIENTS

½ cup extra-virgin olive oil

1 medium onion, chopped

1 carrot, peeled and chopped

2 cloves garlic, chopped

1½ teaspoon Italian seasoning

1 teaspoon unrefined salt

¼ teaspoon black pepper

Pinch red pepper flakes

2 cans (28 ounces/794 grams each) whole, peeled tomatoes

¼ cup fresh basil leaves

1 tablespoon local honey or maple syrup (optional)

INSTRUCTIONS

1. In a large pot, heat olive oil over medium heat.
2. Add onions and carrot, and cook until onions are very soft, about 5 minutes.
3. Stir in garlic, Italian seasonings, salt, black pepper and red pepper flakes and cook for 2 to 3 additional minutes.
4. Add tomatoes. Bring to a boil, reduce heat to low, and let simmer, uncovered, for 30 minutes.
5. Turn off heat, stir in basil, and allow to cool for a few minutes.
6. Blend the sauce until smooth, in batches if necessary.
7. Taste the sauce. If it tastes slightly acidic, add the honey or maple syrup and blend again.
8. Use immediately or store in the refrigerate for up to 4 days or in the freezer for up to 3 months.

YOGURT TARTAR SAUCE

YIELD ½ cup

PREP 5 minutes   TOTAL 5 minutes

Ⓝ NUT-FREE

This is a flavorful tartar sauce made with yogurt instead of mayonnaise. Add finely diced pickles for a more authentic tartar sauce or make it smooth by using pickle juice only.

INGREDIENTS

½ cup plain Greek, whole milk or non-dairy yogurt
2 tablespoons fresh lemon juice
2 tablespoons pickle juice
¼ teaspoon unrefined salt
⅛ teaspoon ground black pepper
1 pickle, finely diced (optional)

INSTRUCTIONS

1. Combine yogurt, lemon juice, pickle juice, salt, black pepper and diced pickles if using in a small bowl and mix to combine.
2. Use immediately or transfer sauce to an airtight container and refrigerate.

VEGAN 'PARMESAN'

YIELD 1 cup

PREP 3 minutes   TOTAL 3 minutes

You will be surprised by how this 'Parmesan' made using cashews actually tastes like cheese. It has a creamy, salty and cheesy taste, so give it a try! Use it to sprinkle on salads, pasta or casseroles.

INGREDIENTS

1 cup raw cashews
3 tablespoons nutritional yeast
¾ teaspoon garlic powder
½ teaspoon unrefined salt

INSTRUCTIONS

1. Place cashews in a food processor along with the nutritional yeast, garlic powder and salt. Process until mostly smooth.
2. Use immediately or store in a glass container in the refrigerator. It will last several weeks.

TAHINI SAUCE

YIELD 1 cups

PREP 5 minutes   TOTAL 5 minutes

Ⓘ NUT-FREE

This is a perfect sauce to eat with falafels. It can also be used in salads or Buddha bowls.

INGREDIENTS

¼ cup tahini
2 tablespoons sesame or extra-virgin olive oil
½ cup filtered water
2 tablespoons fresh lemon juice
¼ teaspoon unrefined salt

INSTRUCTIONS

1. Combine tahini, oil, water, lemon juice and salt in a blender and blend until smooth.
2. Use immediately or refrigerate until ready to use. You may, however, need to add a little water to thin it out.

WEEKLY MENU IDEAS

WEEK 1 – SPRING/SUMMER

	BREAKFAST	LUNCH	DINNER
MONDAY	Acai Bowl	Rainbow Pasta Salad	Zucchini Fritters
TUESDAY	Bircher Muesli	Sandwich and Coleslaw with Apples	Baked Salmon with Fresh Herbs
WEDNESDAY	Blueberry Pie Smoothie	Sandwich with Avocado Egg Salad	Minestrone with Quinoa and Kale
THURSDAY	Overnight Cream of Oats	Kale Salad	Lemon Thyme Chicken
FRIDAY	Dreamy Strawberry Smoothie	Leftovers	Baked Falafels with Hummus
SATURDAY	Tofu Scramble	Quinoa Salad	Sweet Potato Tuna Patties
SUNDAY	French Toast	Egg Muffins	Chicken Sausage Skillet with Cauliflower Rice

TO BAKE: Blueberry Lemon Cake

WEEK 2 – SPRING/SUMMER

	BREAKFAST	LUNCH	DINNER
MONDAY	Carrot Cake Smoothie	Bean Tuna Salad	Spinach Tofu Lasagna
TUESDAY	Nut-free Granola with Nondairy Milk	Leftovers	Crispy Fish Cakes with Coleslaw with Apples
WEDNESDAY	Chia Pudding	Wrap with Avocado Egg Salad	Loaded Sweet Potatoes
THURSDAY	Amaranth Porridge	Avocado Toasts	Chicken Tenders with Honey Mustard Dipping Sauce
FRIDAY	Hulk Smoothie	Southwest Scrambled Eggs	Spaghetti with Avocado Basil Sauce
SATURDAY	Acai Bowl	Tofu Scramble	Pan-seared Salmon with Avocado Mango Salsa
SUNDAY	Buckwheat Raspberry Pancakes	Egg Muffins	Greek-style Lamb Kebabs with Salad and Tzatziki Sauce

TO MAKE: Banana Ice Cream and Raspberry Sorbet

WEEK 1 – FALL/WINTER

	BREAKFAST	LUNCH	DINNER
MONDAY	Chia Pudding	Wild Rice Salad	Cream of Broccoli Soup
TUESDAY	Old-fashioned Oatmeal	Leftovers	Sheet-pan Honey Dijon Chicken
WEDNESDAY	Raspberry Oat Smoothie	Mexican Bean Salad	Cod Leek Potato Casserole
THURSDAY	Amaranth Porridge	Avocado Toasts	Teriyaki Tofu and Broccoli
FRIDAY	Cookie Dough Smoothie	Chickpea Salad	Turkey Meatballs with Mashed Cauliflower
SATURDAY	Baked Oatmeal	Kale Salad	Rainbow Trout with Spinach and Sweet Potato Purée
SUNDAY	Bircher Muesli	Eggs Benedict	Pasta with Mom's Spaghetti Sauce

TO BAKE: Banana Bread

WEEK 2 – FALL/WINTER

	BREAKFAST	LUNCH	DINNER
MONDAY	Chocolate Hazelnut Smoothie	Leftovers	Veggie Burger with Sweet Potato Fries
TUESDAY	Overnight Cream of Oats	Sandwich with Avocado Egg Salad	Sole Meuniere with Garlicky Green Beans
WEDNESDAY	Creamy Peanut Butter Smoothie	Avocado Toasts	Glazed Maple Soy Chicken Thighs with Rice and Broccoli
THURSDAY	Apple Cinnamon Oatmeal	Leftovers	Thai Red Curry Ground Beef
FRIDAY	Nut-free Granola with Nondairy Milk	Chicken Waldorf Salad	Potato Leek Soup
SATURDAY	Bircher Muesli	Healthy 'Mac N' Cheese'	Almond-Crusted Cod with Brussels Sprouts
SUNDAY	Chia Pudding	Breakfast Hash	Sweet Potato Shepherd's Pie

TO BAKE: Healthy Brownies

PANTRY ESSENTIALS

Here is a shopping list of the ingredients I recommend keeping in your pantry.
If you like, store them in labeled Mason jars.

GRAINS

Rolled oats
Basmati brown rice
Basmati white rice
Jasmine rice
Quinoa
Millet
Amaranth

PASTA

Brown rice or wild rice pasta
Quinoa pasta
Rice noodles
Brown rice lasagna noodles

FLOUR

Almond flour
Buckwheat flour
Coconut flour
Oat flour

STARCHES

Arrowroot starch
Tapioca starch
Organic cornstarch

FATS AND OILS

Extra-virgin olive oil
Coconut oil
Sesame oil
Toasted sesame oil
Flaxseed oil
Grass-fed butter

BEANS AND LEGUMES

Canned chickpeas
Canned black beans
Canned pinto beans
Dried red lentils
Dried green/brown lentils

NUTS AND SEEDS (RAW), AND BUTTERS

Almonds
Cashews
Chia seeds
Flaxseeds
Hemp seeds
Pumpkin seeds
Sesame seeds
Sunflower seeds
Walnuts
Almond butter
Tahini (sesame butter)

SUPERFOODS AND DRIED FRUITS

Coconut flakes, unsweetened
Raw cacao
Goji berries
Raisins

SWEETENERS

Blackstrap molasses
Coconut sugar
Coconut nectar
Medjool dates
Organic honey
Pure maple syrup
Sucanat

DRIED HERBS, SPICES AND SEASONINGS

Bay leaves
Black pepper, ground and peppercorn
Cayenne pepper
Chili powder
Cinnamon
Coriander
Cumin
Curry
Garlic powder
Ginger
Nutmeg
Onion powder
Oregano
Paprika
Red pepper flakes
Smoked paprika
Thyme
Turmeric
Himalayan salt
Wheat-free tamari
Nutritional yeast
Vanilla extract

OTHER

Whole peeled tomatoes
Crushed tomatoes
Tomato paste
Chicken broth, low-sodium
Vegetable broth, low-sodium
Canned coconut milk, full-fat
Dark chocolate chips

CONVERSION CHARTS

OVEN TEMPERATURE

FAHRENHEIT	CELSIUS	GAS MARK
275F	140C	1
300F	150C	2
325F	165C	3
350F	177C	4
375F	190C	5
400F	200C	6
425F	220C	7
450F	230C	8
475F	245C	9
500F	260C	10

U.S. LIQUID VOLUME MEASUREMENTS

MEASUREMENT	EQUIVALENT
8 fluid ounces	1 cup
1 pint	2 cups or 16 fluid ounces
1 quart	2 pints or 4 cups
1 gallon	4 quarts or 16 cups

U.S. TO METRIC CONVERSIONS

MEASUREMENT	EQUIVALENT
1 teaspoon	5 ml
1 tablespoon	15 ml
1 fluid ounce	30 ml
1 cup	240 ml
2 cups or 1 pint	470 ml
4 cups or 1 quart	0.95 liter
4 quarts or 1 gallon	3.8 liters
1 ounce	28 grams
8 ounces or ½ pound	230 grams
16 ounces or 1 pound	454 grams

U.S. DRY VOLUME MEASUREMENTS

MEASUREMENT	EQUIVALENT
¹⁄₁₆ teaspoon	Dash
⅛ teaspoon	Pinch
3 teaspoons	1 tablespoon
⅛ cup	2 tablespoons
¼ cup	4 tablespoons
⅓ cup	5 tablespoons + 1 teaspoon
½ cup	8 tablespoons
1 cup	16 tablespoons
1 pound	16 ounces

ABOUT THE AUTHOR

Krystelle is a wife, mother and stepmother. She is French Canadian and lives in the beautiful city of Montreal. Her passion for holistic health and nutrition started when she was a teenager and realized how food had such a big impact on her body, mind and soul.

At 20, she met her husband and soon became stepmother to three young children, including one with autism. She began learning how to cook for a large family with varying tastes and dietary needs—a challenging venture which gained her valuable cooking experience.

Krystelle studied holistic health and nutrition, and then completed a culinary education in raw vegan cuisine in California and culinary school in New York City. She holds a degree in health coaching, holistic nutrition and culinary arts.

After Krystelle had her first child, she was inspired to start sharing her passion for healthy living and knowledge of healthy cooking with other parents. At home with her young son, she started an online community and created her first cookbook.

Krystelle also loves to travel and has visited more than 35 countries. Her travels helped her discover and appreciate different ingredients, tastes and cuisines from around the world. She now incorporates them into her cooking to create a variety of healthy and flavorful dishes.

Today, her mission is to help and inspire parents to make healthier food choices and cook healthier meals for their family so they can be healthy and enjoy life to its fullest.

You can learn more about her via her website consciouscooking.com.

ACKNOWLEDGMENTS

This book has been a true labor of love and wouldn't have been possible without the support of my friends, family, my team, as well as all the teachers, mentors and education I have had throughout the years.

First and foremost, thank you to my husband, Stephan, for your love, continuous support, generosity, and for always believing in me. Thank you to my son, Noah, and my stepchildren Mathias, Tristan and Sophia for testing and approving (most) of my recipes. Thank you to my sisters, parents and all my friends for your support, humor and love. I feel so blessed to have you all in my life.

Thank you to my photographer, Leila Afraz, for styling and capturing all the beautiful photographs in the book. Thank you to my graphic designer, Julie Hodgins, for your energy and patience, and for having put the book together so beautifully. Thank you to my proofreader, Mark Baker, for your detail-oriented work and dedication, to Amanda Bochain, for having reviewed the book so efficiently, and to Chloe Beaudoin, for having translated the entire book in French. It has been a pleasure to work with you all.

Thank you to my followers on social media for your support, feedback and goodwill, and thank you to my readers for granting me with the opportunity to share my recipes with your families. I truly hope you enjoy them.

Lastly, I would like to acknowledge and recognize the institutions and schools that I had the pleasure to learn from:

- Natural Gourmet Institute – Chef Training Program in New York City, New York

- Canadian School of Natural Nutrition – Holistic Nutrition Program in Toronto, Ontario

- Institute for Integrative Nutrition – Health Coaching Program in New York City, New York

- Living Light Culinary Institute – Raw Food Chef & Instructor Program in Fort Bragg, California

- Hippocrates Health Institute - Health and Educator Program in West Palm Beach, Florida

- Alternative Medicine College of Canada - Natural Health Practitioner Program in Montreal, Quebec

This book has been a true collaboration and it wouldn't have been possible without all of you. From the bottom of my heart, thank you and *merci!*

INDEX